W9-CAW-223

J.K. ROWLING

Author of *Harry Potter*

Karen Leigh Harmin

Enslow Publishers, Inc.
40 Industrial Road
Box 398
Berkeley Heights, NJ 07922
USA

http://www.enslow.com

Library of Congress Cataloging-in-Publication Data

J.K. Rowling : author of Harry Potter / Karen Leigh Harmin.
p. cm. — (People to know today)
Includes bibliographical references and index.
ISBN 0-7660-1850-4 (hardcover)
1. Rowling, J. K. 2. Authors, English—20th century—Biography. 3. Potter, Harry (Fictitious character). 4. Children's stories—Authorship. I. Title. II. Series.
PR6068.O93Z685 2006
823'.914—dc22
[B]

2005020400

Printed in the United States of America

10 9 8 7 6 5 4 3 2 1

To Our Readers: This biography has not been authorized by J. K. Rowling or her agents or assigns, including Warner Bros. Entertainment, Inc. Harry Potter is a trademark of Warner Bros. Entertainment, Inc.

We have done our best to make sure all Internet Addresses in this book were active and appropriate when we went to press. However, the author and the publisher have no control over and assume no liability for the material available on those Internet sites or on other Web sites they may link to. Any comments or suggestions can be sent by e-mail to comments@enslow.com or to the address on the back cover.

Every effort has been made to locate all copyright holders of material used in this book. If any errors or omissions have occurred, corrections will be made in future editions of this book.

Illustration Credits: ©2006 Jupiterimages Corporation, pp. 24, 44; AP/Wide World, pp. 1, 4, 36, 60, 62, 69, 71, 73, 75, 78, 80, 86, 91, 93, 98, 102, 104 (1, 2, 3), 108; AP/Tim Graham, Tim Graham Picture Library, pp. 32, 52, 64; Associated Press, KEYSTONE, p. 104 (4); Associated Press, PAMPC PA, pp. 82, 106; © Corel Corporation, pp. 28, 40; Enslow Publishers, Inc., p. 11; Forest of Dean District Council, p. 17.

Cover Illustrations: AP/Wide World

CONTENTS

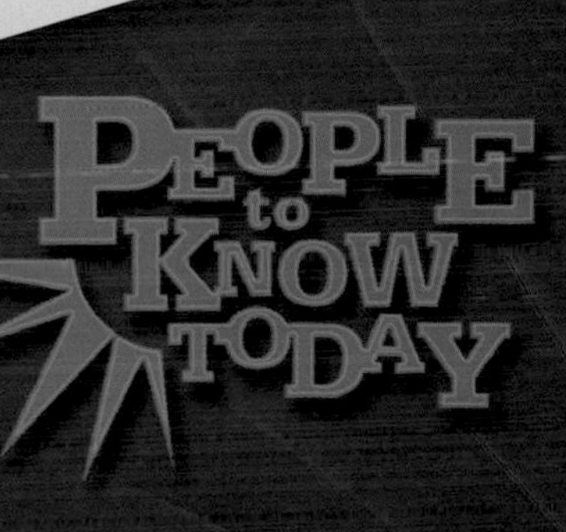

J. K. Rowling was about to go from obscurity to tremendous fame. By the time this photo was taken, in July 2005, Rowling was a beloved author around the world.

1 A WRITER'S DREAM COMES TRUE

It was 8:00 on a June evening in 1997, and Joanne Rowling (pronounced RŌ, as in "row the boat") settled in for a typical night. She planned to read a story to her preschooler, Jessica, put her to bed, and then spend the rest of the evening working on the second book in her *Harry Potter* series. Rowling was still getting used to the idea of becoming a published author. Her first book, *Harry Potter and the Philosopher's Stone*, was about to be published by Bloomsbury, a publishing company in England. At last, her lifelong dream of seeing her writing in print was becoming a reality.

Rowling had lived for nearly a year in poverty, writing her first book while caring for her infant daughter as a single mother. Signing a book contract for *Harry Potter and the Philosopher's Stone* had somewhat eased her financial worries.

She was not paid much money, but for the first time since Jessica was born, Rowling could relax a bit from the strain of keeping track of every penny. Still, she knew that most writers of children's fiction make very little money, and she had not expected *Harry Potter* to change her life. She would earn a small sum for every copy of her book that was sold. If *Harry Potter* found even a small audience, she would no longer be solely dependent on her income as a French teacher.

On that June evening, it seemed to Rowling that her life could not get any better. Then the phone rang. Her literary agent, Christopher Little, was calling from the Bologna Book Fair in Italy. One of the main purposes of this publishing-industry trade fair is for publishers from all over the world to buy international publishing rights. The American rights for *Harry Potter and the Philosopher's Stone* were up for auction that very evening, and the bidding was enthusiastic and intense.

It seemed to Rowling that her life could not get any better.

Rowling was astonished at the news. She had never really considered the possibility that *Harry Potter* would be published outside the United Kingdom. She had worked so hard on finding an English publisher to buy her book that she had not put any effort into dreaming about what would happen next.

Christopher Little reported that the bidding was already up to five figures (between $10,000 and $99,000). "I went cold with shock," Rowling said.[1] The first advance payment from her English publisher, Bloomsbury, had been only £2,000 (about $3,200). It seemed impossible that the Americans could be bidding so hard for the right to publish *Harry Potter* in the United States. Rowling hung up the phone so that Little could get back to the auction floor.

Little called again at 10 P.M. to say that the bidding was now up to six figures (more than $100,000).

> *I put down the telephone to my agent, Christopher, in a state of advanced shock (I think my contribution to the conversation consisted almost entirely of the words 'How much? I don't believe it'), walked around my flat for hours in a kind of nervous frenzy, and went to bed at about 2 A.M.*[2]

At 11 P.M., Rowling received a call from Arthur Levine, an editor at the American publisher Scholastic, Inc. "The first words he said to me were: 'Don't panic.' "[3]

The Business of Books

Book publishers work hard to sell the rights to publish their books in other languages and in other media. This includes international editions that are published in other countries and other languages—as well as permission to create movies, television shows, or even action figures or board games based on a book or its characters. Publishers make a great deal of money from these "subsidiary rights." Authors, too, can earn extra money when their book is published in other countries or made into a movie or a toy.

Levine had big news: Scholastic had won the auction—and the American rights for *Harry Potter and the Philosopher's Stone* had been sold for $105,000, more than ten times the typical rate for a children's book. Rowling was to receive more money than had ever been paid for a children's book in the history of American publishing.[4]

Arthur Levine said that after reading an advance copy of *Harry Potter*, he had fallen so in love with it that he was determined to be the book's United States publisher, no matter what the cost. Rowling's life had just changed forever. It was not just the money, although the huge sum would make a big difference in the life of a struggling single mother. More important, the success of the auction meant that Harry Potter would become a citizen, not just of the United Kingdom, but of the world.

Joanne Rowling was on her way to becoming one of the best-known, best-loved children's writers in the history of publishing.

2 A House Full of Books

Joanne Rowling, known as Jo, was born into a family of readers and story lovers. Her parents, Pete Rowling and Anne Volant, had met in 1964 on a train traveling from London to Scotland. Both were eighteen years old. Pete Rowling, an Englishman, had recently joined the British navy. Anne Volant, half-Scottish and half-English, had also just entered the military. She was a member of the Women's Royal Naval Service (known as WREN), a group that did noncombat jobs in the navy.

Anne and Pete were both returning to their navy base in Scotland. The train compartment was full of WRENs, but Pete pushed passed the others to sit next to Anne. For Anne, it was love at first sight. The two became instantly absorbed in conversation as if they had known each other all their lives.

By the time Pete and Anne got off the train a few hours later in Scotland, they were already a couple. They were married the next year on March 14, 1965, at All Saints Parish Church in Tufnell Park, near London.[1] They both left the military to start their lives together as civilians. Pete chose to follow in his father's footsteps and become a machinist. When he landed a training position at an aircraft factory near Bristol, the young couple moved into their first house in the small town of Yate.[2]

Joanne Rowling was born on July 31, 1965, at Cottage Hospital in Yate.[3] (She sometimes says that she was born in Chipping Sodbury—a nearby town with a great name—but her birth certificate reveals that she was really born in Yate.)

Jo's first two years were spent at home with her mother in Sundridge Park, a neighborhood in Yate. The Rowlings' home was surrounded by open fields. Yate had the feel of a market town, where local farmers would bring their crops and livestock to sell on market day. But it was slowly changing from an old-fashioned English village into a modern, working-class town. Within a year or two of Jo's birth, a shopping mall was built within walking distance of their house. The Rowlings did not like these changes in their community. They thought Yate was becoming too suburban.

A second daughter, Dianne, was born on June 28, 1967. Instead of going to the hospital to give birth,

Anne Rowling decided to have this baby at home. Jo, not quite two years old, was present for the arrival of the doctor, the rush of preparations, and the flow of people in and out of the house as the birth grew near. To keep Jo busy and out of trouble, her father gave her some playdough. Years later, she would have no memory at all of the birth or of seeing her sister for the first time, but she would remember eating the playdough.[4]

After Dianne was born, Pete Rowling finished his training at the aircraft factory and was given a permanent job with a bigger salary. Because they now had

Jo has lived in various parts of Great Britain over the years.

two children and needed more room, the Rowlings moved into a bigger home at 35 Nicholls Lane in Winterbourne. It was only four miles from Yate, but the neighborhood felt completely different. Winterbourne was still a farming community. The Rowlings' new home looked out on meadows, and a blacksmith's forge operated nearby.

Pete Rowling continued to work at the aircraft factory in Bristol. The factory had been purchased by Rolls-Royce, a company most famous for manufacturing luxury cars. Rolls-Royce was also known for building first-rate engines for fighter jets. Pete worked on jet engines, becoming so skilled that he soon left assembly work behind and was promoted into management.

Anne Rowling stayed at home to raise her children. In the 1960s, it was unusual for mothers of young children to work outside the home, so in this way the Rowlings were a typical Winterbourne family. And because this was the era before modern kitchen conveniences—there were no dishwashers, microwave ovens, or ready-made dinners—there was a great deal of work to keep a young wife and mother busy.

In spite of the housework that constantly needed to be done, Anne Rowling made something else her top priority: books. She was a tireless, enthusiastic reader, and she made certain that the Rowling household was filled with books.

Pete Rowling also encouraged his daughters' love of books. When Jo was sick in bed with the measles, he helped her pass the hours of boredom and discomfort by reading from *The Wind in the Willows*, by Kenneth Grahame. The stories of Mr. Toad and Badger came alive in the sound of her father's voice. The itchiness of the measles quickly faded, but *The Wind in the Willows* remains in her memory to this day.

Books were a top priority in the Rowling household.

A passion for books helped cement Anne Rowling's friendship with her neighbor Ruby Potter. The Potters had two children very close in age to Jo and Dianne. Ian and Vikki Potter became constant companions of the Rowling sisters. The four children played games in the front yard as their mothers sat and talked about books. At a time when video games and personal computers were barely imagined, and in a community where television was rarely found in working-class homes, books were a good source of entertainment for families and could help forge bonds between friends.

Jo soon drafted her sister, Dianne, and the Potter children into a variety of make-believe games that gave a hint of what lay in the future. Jo became the ringleader not simply because she was the oldest, but because she had already developed a love of storytelling. She constructed elaborate fantasies that sent everyone rifling through boxes of dress-up clothing for costumes and props.[5]

When Jo turned five, her parents enrolled her in the nearby school at St. Michael's Church of England. On the first day of school, Jo's mother walked her to St. Michael's and left her there. Apparently no one explained to young Jo that this would be her routine for many days and years to come. Jo happily joined the class under the impression that school lasted only one day. She was quite shocked to learn that she would be going to St. Michael's every day.[6] Still, she enjoyed school and the pottery making, drawing, and writing she did there.

Jo attended St. Michael's School for the next three years. In 1974, when Jo was nine, her family decided to move again. The area around Bristol was growing rapidly, and Winterbourne was changing from a quiet farm community into a bustling suburb. The Rowlings had been exploring the area for some time and decided that Tutshill, a charming little village on the border of England and Wales, would be the best place to raise their daughters.

Driving through Tutshill one day, Anne and Pete discovered that Church Cottage was on the market. It was just what they wanted. Church Cottage, built in 1848, had served as the first

Jo's First Story

When Jo was five or six, she wrote her first story. It was about a rabbit named Rabbit. He gets the measles, and his friends, including Miss Bee, come to visit. After that, Jo knew that her secret wish was to become a writer.

schoolroom and church in the area, until a larger church was built in 1853. The cottage had continued as the local schoolroom until 1893, when a new school was built and the cottage was turned into a home. The creaky old structure, with its rough stone floors, old-fashioned windows, and many other original features from 1853, was not a typical suburban house. It was the perfect home to fuel the imagination of a young storyteller.

For Jo, switching to a new school turned out to be a bit traumatic. The administrators of the Tutshill Church of England School believed in creating a strict and disciplined place for children. Particularly difficult was Jo's first teacher, Mrs. Sylvia Morgan. Many students were so afraid of her that they started crying even before entering her class for the first time.

It was the perfect home to fuel the imagination of a young storyteller.

Mrs. Morgan had a system for sorting the students in her class: On the first day she gave an arithmetic test, then used the results to decide who was intelligent and who was "dim," as Jo said.[7] On the day that Jo took the test, Mrs. Morgan asked questions about fractions, which Jo had never seen before. When Jo scored a half point out of a possible ten points on the test, she was seated in the row of dim students.

During her first few weeks of school, Jo made new

friends. Then she realized that she had been grouped with the less-intelligent students. After that, she concentrated on earning a seat near the brighter students. She worked harder than ever at her schoolwork, becoming a bossy know-it-all not unlike a character she would one day create—Hermione Granger in *Harry Potter.*

Jo's social status changed on the day that Mrs. Morgan moved her into the row with the best students: By swapping Jo's seat with that of her best friend, Mrs. Morgan ensured that Jo would now be unpopular. One day in the future, Jo's character Hermione Granger would find herself having a similar experience at Hogwart's.[8]

Without a group of friends to pass her time with, Jo spent much of her first years in Tutshill exploring the countryside with her sister, Dianne. Tutshill sat on the River Wye, near the Forest of Dean, an ancient and beautiful forest that has inspired myths and legends for centuries. Wandering through the Forest of Dean, long considered special and magical, young Jo could create characters and imagine fanciful stories.

"I was shy. I was a mixture of insecurities and very bossy. Very bossy to my sister but quite quiet with strangers."[9]

Jo also had plenty of time to indulge her passion for books. She read everything she could find. As a young child

As a girl, Jo spent hours exploring the Forest of Dean, with her imagination running wild.

she had loved the stories of Richard Scarry, but now she was reading books by Edith Nesbit and Enid Blyton, along with the *Chronicles of Narnia* by C. S. Lewis. She became a devoted fan of Jane Austen's novels, especially *Pride and Prejudice* and *Emma* (she eventually reread *Emma* more than twenty times).[10]

Jo's life changed again at age eleven, when she began attending secondary school. The Wyedean Comprehensive Secondary School was a state-run school located in the town of Sedbury, two miles from her home.

As she approached her teens, Jo's interests were expanding beyond her own little world. She was becoming politically aware. When she was fourteen, Jo read *Hons and Rebels*, Jessica Mitford's memoir of her political activism during the early 1900s. Mitford describes growing up in an aristocratic English household in the early twentieth century and running away to live a more political, less conventional life. Jo admired Mitford's sense of individualism and courage in the face of political oppression.[11]

Jo said, "My sister and I both, we were that kind of teenager. (Dripping with drama.) We were that kind of, 'I'm the only one who really feels these injustices. No one else understands the way I feel.' I think a lot of teenagers go through that."[12]

Also like so many teenagers, Jo became more concerned with popularity than with schoolwork. Although she had been an excellent student up until this point, she had also learned a hard lesson about being a secondary-school student in England in 1976: If you were a girl and a top student, it was very difficult to be popular as well.

The British School System

Children in the United Kingdom enter primary school at age five. At eleven, they move up to secondary school. By law, they must stay in school until they turn sixteen, but students aiming for a university education spend seven years in secondary school, graduating at age eighteen. Sixteen-year-old students take several exams (which were called Ordinary levels—"O levels"—when Rowling was in school). Passing five of these exams qualified Rowling to take Advanced levels—"A levels"—additional exams required by many universities.

This testing tradition is echoed in the *Harry Potter* books: Fifth-year students must take OWLs (Ordinary Wizarding Level exams), while seventh-year students may elect to take NEWTs (Nastily Exhausting Wizarding Tests).

With her high grades, Jo occasionally had to deal with taunts and insults from other students. She was even subjected to physical bullying, such as pushing and shoving in the hallways.

Wyedean also held some very positive experiences for Jo. She was given formal training in creative writing for the first time. Her creative-writing teacher, twenty-year-old Lucy Shepherd, demanded effort and focus from her students. Jo took the class very seriously and began writing regularly. She greatly admired Lucy Shepherd, but did not reveal her dreams of becoming a writer.[13]

Because Tutshill was such a small village, there was no outside entertainment for teenagers—no movie theater, no clubs, no concert halls. Teenagers socialized outside school by meeting at one another's homes or hanging out on street corners. During her first few years of secondary school, Jo spent most of her free time writing stories in her bedroom.

Jo wrote lots of stories as a teen, but she rarely showed them to her friends.

When Jo was about fourteen, she saw the movie *Grease.* Jo immediately identified with the bad-girl character of Rizzo. To look like Rizzo, she started wearing heavy eye makeup and a denim jacket. She developed a tough-girl appearance and became more open about smoking cigarettes. She also started listening to punk rock music, which was quite new at this time.[14]

One unexpected advantage to Jo's new image was that it helped her handle the bullying at school. Identifying with the streetwise Rizzo gave Jo the emotional strength to fight back instead of running away. When a girl attacked her one day, Jo managed to fight her off. Later, Jo downplayed her newfound courage: "I didn't have a choice. It was hit back or lie down and play dead. For a few days I was quite famous because she hadn't managed to flatten me. The truth was, my locker was right behind me and it held me up."[15]

In 1980, when Jo was fifteen years old, her mother was diagnosed with multiple sclerosis. Anne Rowling had an unusually aggressive form of the disease. She had first noticed symptoms in 1978, when she sometimes found herself unable to pour tea because her hand was shaking too much to hold the teapot. She soon had trouble lifting things and became prone to breaking glass beakers in the chemistry lab at Wyedean Secondary School. She was working there as a lab assistant.

After she was diagnosed, Anne had to give up her job in the chemistry lab, but she was not willing to stay home and do nothing. As long as she was able to get out of the house, she kept herself busy by volunteering to clean the local church. After a few weeks, she became so weak that volunteering was no longer possible. Moving around became so difficult that she was reduced to crawling up the stairs of her home. Shortly after that, she was confined to a wheelchair.

Jo found it extremely hard to watch her mother deteriorate so quickly. She left the house whenever she could, but Tutshill was too small and offered no place to escape from the tragedy unfolding at home. As a result, Jo threw herself more and more into her writing, her interest in alternative music, and the Goth scene, which was becoming increasingly popular among English teenagers.

Jo was saved from depression during her last year in secondary school by the arrival of a new student, Sean Harris. Sean's father served in the British army, and his family often moved. So Sean was used to being uprooted and changing schools. Sean and Jo quickly became friends because they both felt like outsiders in Tutshill. They also shared an interest in alternative music and political activism. Sean had his driver's license and an old Ford Anglia, which meant that he and Jo could finally escape

Multiple Sclerosis

Commonly known as MS, multiple sclerosis is an illness of the central nervous system. It interferes with communication between the brain and the muscles. A person suffering from MS can become very weak and may even lose the ability to walk. MS can take several forms: Some patients live for many years without getting worse, while others rapidly become disabled. There is no cure for MS, and research has yet to find an effective treatment for the aggressive forms of the disease.

from Tutshill for a few hours. (This car was later given a role in *Harry Potter and the Chamber of Secrets* as the Weasleys' enchanted car.) Jo and Sean would occasionally drive into the nearby cities of Bristol, Cardiff, and Bath to hear music in clubs and discos. More often, they would simply drive to nearby Severn Bridge and sit under the bridge for hours, talking about their futures.

In spite of the tragedy of her mother's illness, and perhaps because she had a sympathetic ear in her friend Sean, Jo managed to stabilize her life and studies enough to become head girl, or lead student, at Wyedean. Unlike the head girl position at Hogwarts in the *Harry Potter* books, the Wyedean position was an elected one, voted on by both faculty and students. This meant that Jo had to be a good enough student to earn faculty votes, and popular enough with other students to win their votes, too. The position

The Goth Scene

Goth began in England around 1979 as an outgrowth of the punk rock movement. The first well-known Goth band was Siouxsie and the Banshees. By 1983 Goth had become a subculture, identified not just by music but by a distinctive style of dress featuring elaborate black costumes. Women often wear corsets and veils, and men's apparel includes ruffled shirts and large buckles. Women also apply heavy makeup, especially eyeliner, and tease their hair. Both men and women wear a lot of jewelry and accessories, usually in silver or pewter.

was mostly honorary and took little time or effort by Jo.

The teachers at Wyedean, recognizing Jo's intelligence and talent, encouraged her to apply to Oxford University, one of the most prestigious schools in the world. Jo took Oxford's entrance exams in English, French, and German. Although she scored top marks in English and French, and good marks in German, she was not accepted. Instead Jo would attend the University of Exeter. In the fall of 1983, she finally left Tutshill and entered the larger world, traveling to Exeter by train to begin her university education.

Rowling did more socializing than studying at the University of Exeter.

3 Becoming a Storyteller

The **University of Exeter** began as a collection of small schools and colleges in rural England in the middle of the nineteenth century. By the time Rowling started classes there in 1983, it had become a large, modern university with several thousand students. The campus has the reputation of being one of the most beautiful in England. Its hilly location offers striking views of the surrounding countryside and of the university's gardens of rare trees and flowers.

More important for Rowling was the fact that Exeter was relatively close to home. The university was only a couple of hours from Tutshill, so she could easily visit her parents and sister. She had not yet learned how to drive a car, but the train stations were not far from the university and the Rowling home.

With her secret dream of becoming a writer, Rowling wanted to study English literature. Her parents discouraged her from making this choice, arguing that a degree in English literature would not give her any marketable job skills for the future. They urged her to study languages, particularly French. They hoped that she would become an interpreter or a bilingual secretary after she finished school. Rowling half-heartedly took her parents' advice, enrolling in French and classics (Latin and Greek) courses during her first year at Exeter. "I had succumbed to parental pressure to study 'useful' modern languages as opposed to 'but-where-will-it-lead?' English and really should have stood my ground."[1]

With her secret dream of becoming a writer, Rowling wanted to study English literature, but her parents discouraged her.

From the start, it was obvious that Rowling was interested less in her studies than in the other aspects of university life. She had some trouble settling in: "At first Exeter was a bit of a shock. I was expecting to be among lots of similar people—thinking radical thoughts. But it wasn't like that. However, once I'd made friends with some like-minded people, I began to enjoy myself."[2]

Rowling's first two years of study were uneventful.

Like all students, she attended lectures and completed assignments. However, her heart was clearly not in her work. Rowling later commented on one professor's willingness to put up with her mediocre performance:

> *His tolerance towards my frightening ignorance of his subject was awe-inspiring. The closest he ever came to admonishing me for my erratic attendance and propensity to lose every handout he gave me the moment we parted company was when he described me as sleepwalking around the place.*[3]

While she did her work well enough to get by, Rowling's real energy went into her social life. She and her circle of friends were a regular presence at Devonshire House, the student center. They spent countless hours there, drinking coffee and socializing. Rowling was known for making up entertaining stories that cast her friends as characters.

Toward the end of her second year at Exeter, Rowling's inattention to her studies caught up with her. Her adviser persuaded her to drop her courses in classics and to concentrate solely on French.

As a French major, Rowling was required to spend a year abroad to improve her language skills. She was given a choice: teach English in a French school, study at a French university, or work for a French company. Rowling decided to teach English part-time in Paris.

Rowling taught English in France for her junior year of college.

Sharing an apartment in Paris with an Italian, a Spaniard, and a Russian turned out to be an interesting and varied cultural experience. Rowling also got her first exposure to teaching languages, a job she would qualify for after graduation. Whenever she had free time, she spent it locked in her bedroom reading great works of literature, such as Charles Dickens's *A Tale of Two Cities.*

In the fall of 1986, Rowling returned to Exeter for her final year of college. Before graduating, she had to write a three-thousand-word paper in French.[4] She finished all her work and in June 1987 graduated from the University of Exeter. Her grades were average, but not exceptional. Rowling was the first member of her family to earn a university degree, and her parents proudly watched as she crossed the stage to accept her diploma on graduation day.[5] By this time, her mother was confined to a wheelchair.

Her formal education completed, Jo now faced the challenge of most college graduates: finding a job. Anne and Pete Rowling offered advice, just as they had about her college major. They suggested that their daughter move to London and take a course to learn typing, filing, and other office work so that she could find a job as a bilingual secretary. Rowling signed up for a secretarial course, although she knew this career choice might be a mistake: "I was—am—totally unsuited to that kind of work. Me as a secretary? I'd be your worst nightmare."[6]

However boring it might have been for Rowling, learning secretarial skills gave her the ability to earn a living. For the next few years, she lived with various friends from her Exeter days and held a series of part-time or temporary secretarial jobs. She worked for the longest time—about two years—at Amnesty International, where she researched human rights violations in French-speaking parts of Africa. Amnesty International is a worldwide organization that strives to obtain the basic rights of life, liberty, and safety for all people.

While it appeared that Rowling was leading an unfocused, rootless life—never staying in one place or at one job for any length of time—in reality, she had begun to work seriously and privately toward her goal of becoming a writer. She started a novel, writing constantly in her free time. Then, unhappy with that novel, she began a second. She was so focused on her writing that she often secretly used her time at work to write. She would put on the earphones of the office dictating equipment, listen to classical music instead of her employers' dictated notes, and proceed to write stories rather than type up office documents.[7] She put no effort into getting to know her coworkers and made little impression on them. Instead of joining other people for lunch or for drinks after work, she preferred to be alone, writing.

In 1990 Rowling's boyfriend moved to Manchester, a large city several hours north of London. Rowling began spending many hours on the train, traveling between the two cities for weekend visits. On one trip, the train was delayed for several hours. As Rowling sat daydreaming, a stream of images began to play across her imagination—and Harry Potter was born.

All of a sudden the idea for Harry just appeared in my mind's eye. I can't tell you why or what triggered it. But I saw the idea of Harry and the wizard school very plainly. I suddenly had this basic idea of a boy who didn't know who he was, who didn't know he was a wizard until he got his invitation to wizard school. I have never been so excited by an idea.[8]

The train did not move for four hours. Rowling just sat there, as ideas for Harry Potter flooded her mind. She was upset to realize that she had no pen with her. Being too shy to borrow one, she could not write down any of her ideas.

I think that perhaps if I had had to slow down the ideas so that I could capture them on paper I might have stifled some of them (although sometimes I do wonder, idly, how much of what I imagined on that journey I had forgotten by the time I actually got my hands on a pen).[9]

By the end of that train trip, Rowling knew that Harry's story would be a seven-book series, each book covering a year of his time at Hogwarts School of Witchcraft and Wizardry. She had also created Harry's friend Ron Weasley and the Hogwarts caretaker, Rubeus Hagrid. "Hogwarts School of Witchcraft and Wizardry was the first thing I concentrated on. I was thinking of a place of great order but immense danger, with children who had skills with which they could overwhelm their teachers."[10]

When Rowling finally made it back to her apartment that evening, she wrote down all her ideas "in a

Rowling was stuck on a train when Harry Potter appeared in her imagination.

tiny cheap notebook," she said.[11] She also began to write the first few pages of the story that would become *Harry Potter and the Philosopher's Stone*, although those pages were never used in the final version of the book.[12] The very night that Harry Potter crept into her imagination, Rowling began the long process of creating the elaborate and detailed world of Harry and his friends.

Rowling soon moved from London to Manchester to join her boyfriend. She continued living as she had before: working at a series of low-paying secretarial jobs and spending as much of her free time as possible on her writing. However, instead of concentrating on her earlier two novels, she was now consumed by a single project: *Harry Potter*. Inspiration for the story came to her unpredictably. For example, she invented the sport of quidditch—with all of its rules and details—in a single evening, having stormed out of the apartment after an argument with her boyfriend.

On December 30, 1990, after ten years of struggling with MS, Rowling's mother died. Jo had just been home for the holidays, and then left to join friends for a New Year's weekend celebration in the country. She had not known her mother was so near death. In fact, the two of them had just spoken the night before.[13] For Jo, the news came as a great shock:

> *It was a terrible time. My father, Di and I were devastated; she was only forty-five years old and we had never imagined—probably because we could not bear to contemplate the idea—that she could die so young. I remember feeling as though there was a paving slab pressing down upon my chest, a literal pain in my heart.*[14]

A memorial service was held for Anne Rowling in the first week of 1991. When Jo returned to her life in Manchester, she was overwhelmed by grief. Although it seemed that life could not get much unhappier for her, Rowling encountered even more difficulties. The already rocky relationship with her boyfriend started to fall apart, and they argued more and more frequently.

Then her apartment was robbed, and the thieves took everything that Rowling had just inherited from her mother.[15]

Rowling felt that she needed a change in her life. Searching through the help-wanted pages in the *Guardian* newspaper, she found an ad looking for English teachers at Encounter English Schools in Oporto, Portugal. Her experience teaching English in Paris during her third year at Exeter qualified her for the position, and after an interview with the school principal, Steve Cassidy, she was hired.[16]

In November 1991 Rowling flew to Portugal to begin the next chapter of her life. She took along her few possessions, including the stacks of notes she had accumulated over the past six months—all her ideas for *Harry Potter.*

4 Holding Fast to Harry Potter

For Rowling, adjusting to her new life in Portugal was quite easy, thanks to the housing provided by the Encounter English School. Rowling was given an apartment to share with two other teachers, Aine Kiely from Ireland and Jill Prewett from England. The three women, all unmarried and about the same age, found they had many things in common and became close friends.

Rowling taught a variety of students: "They were mostly teenagers preparing for exams but there were also business people and housewives. The teenagers aged between 14 and 17 years were easily my favourite. They were so full of ideas and possibilities, forming opinions."[1] Classes were usually held between 5 P.M. and 10 P.M. and occasionally on weekend mornings. This left Rowling

The city of Oporto, Portugal, is located on the Douro River, near the Atlantic Ocean.

free to spend her days working on *Harry Potter*, either typing on the school computer, or sitting at a nearby café, writing longhand on a pad of paper.

"In my first weeks in Portugal," she said, "I wrote my favourite chapter in *Philosopher's Stone*, The Mirror of Erised."[2] This chapter, in which Harry sees his dead parents in a magical mirror, allowed Rowling to pour out her feelings of grief for her own dead mother. She believes it is one of the most emotional chapters in any of the *Harry Potter* books.

After their classes were done for the day, the three teachers would often head over to a local dance club known as Swing. It was a popular spot for people in their early twenties, and it was also a safe place for three single women to have a drink, listen to music, and dance. Rowling and her roommates spent many free evenings there.

Life continued in a pleasant cycle of work, friendship, and writing until March 1992. One Saturday night, Rowling and her friends were at a local bar, the Meia Cava. The room was full, and among the customers was a young journalism student, Jorge Arantes. Rowling and Arantes were immediately drawn to each other. They began dating, and five months later, in August 1992, Arantes proposed to Rowling. On October 16, 1992, they were married at the civil register office in Oporto. Rowling's sister, Dianne, and her boyfriend flew in from Edinburgh to attend the wedding.[3]

Their marriage turned an emotional relationship into a stormy one. The couple already had a reputation for having passionate public arguments. These scenes grew more frequent and more intense after they were married. Then Jo became pregnant within weeks of the wedding, adding to the couple's stress. She coped by spending more time in cafés and devoting herself to working on *Harry Potter*.

On July 27, 1993, Rowling

Rowling's Approach to Writing

"I have a very visual imagination," says Rowling. "I see a situation and then I try to describe it as vividly as I can. And I do love writing dialog. Dialog comes to me as though I'm just overhearing a conversation."[4]

gave birth to a daughter, Jessica. She was named after Rowling's lifelong hero, the author Jessica Mitford. Although the baby was healthy at birth, she soon developed medical problems and had to stay in the hospital for nearly a month. The strain of having a hospitalized newborn continued to erode the marriage. Tension at home was made worse by the fact that Arantes was not working, leaving Rowling as the sole financial support of their small family.

By their first wedding anniversary, the marriage was in serious trouble. On November 17, 1993, the marriage came to an end with a final explosive argument. Arantes dragged Rowling out of their home in the early hours of the morning and locked her out. He left her standing in the street, their daughter Jessica locked inside with Arantes. Rowling called on the friends who were as close as family to her: Aine Kiely and Jill Prewett. Her former roommates phoned the police, finally persuading them to come and help Rowling get her baby from Arantes.

Under Portuguese law, this was not considered a police matter, and Arantes had no obligation to give his daughter to his wife. Luckily for Rowling, the police intervention was a success: Arantes handed over baby Jessica to be returned to her mother.[5]

Rowling knew that she needed to leave Portugal and get back to the United Kingdom as quickly as possible. She remained in hiding with Jessica for the next two weeks while she made decisions about what to do next. She decided to settle in Edinburgh, Scotland, mostly because her sister, Dianne, lived there. Rowling had always felt great affection for Scotland because it was where her parents had fallen in love. In December 1993, she and Jessica headed for Edinburgh.

It was frightening for Rowling to arrive in Edinburgh as a single mother with an infant, hardly any money, and a dream of becoming a writer. Dianne, who was a lawyer, and her husband, Roger Moore, a businessman, gave Jo and Jessica a home when they first arrived in Edinburgh. But Rowling had no intention of imposing on the newlywed couple any longer than necessary. She quickly came up with a plan:

> *I knew perfectly well that I was walking into poverty, but I truly believed that it would be a matter of months before I was back on my feet. I had enough money saved to put down a deposit on a rented flat and buy a high chair, cot, and other essentials.*[6]

The truth was that Rowling was so short of money that the deposit for her flat came from her old friend Sean Harris, and the furnishings were contributed by other concerned friends.[7]

Rowling had intended to get a teaching job in Edinburgh. But there was a problem: She did not have

Rowling took baby Jessica and fled to the city of Edinburgh, Scotland.

the proper certification to teach school in the United Kingdom. If she could not teach, how would she support herself and Jessica? She needed to earn enough money to pay her household bills as well as day-care expenses while she was at work. A secretarial salary would not be enough.

The government had an assistance program (known as "the dole" in the United Kingdom and "welfare" in the United States) to help people in need. Rowling was considered poor enough to get government aid for her living expenses, but not for day care for Jessica. Working would provide her with even less money—because the government would reduce its aid and she would have the additional burden of child-care payments.

Rowling decided that her only real option was to stay home with Jessica and accept government help. She planned to earn her teacher certification, but even before that, she was determined to finish writing her first *Harry Potter* book:

> *I intended to start teaching again and knew that unless I finished the book very soon, I might never finish it; I knew that full-time teaching, with all the marking and lesson planning, let alone with a small daughter to care for single-handedly, would leave me with absolutely no spare time at all.*[8]

For the next few months, Rowling and her baby lived in poverty. It was one of the lowest points in Rowling's life. Jessica was nourished and warm, but there was barely any money left over for anything else. Occasionally, Rowling bought clothing at second-hand stores, but saving for food was more important. Just getting by was a constant struggle.

Although Rowling adored her daughter and was thrilled to be a mother, the pressure and anxiety of trying to keep her little family afloat was taking its toll on her spirits. Rowling became clinically depressed, convinced that she had made a mess of her life and that she was, as she put it, "a waste of space."[9]

To make matters worse, in March 1994 she heard that Jorge Arantes had come to Edinburgh to find his family. Rowling had not seen her husband since the night of their last fight—when he had thrown her violently out of the house—and she had no wish to see him now. In fact, she was so worried about her own and Jessica's physical safety that she went to court and obtained a restraining order against him. This document stated that Arantes was prohibited from "molesting, abusing [Rowling] verbally, threatening her or putting her in a state of fear and alarm by using violence towards her anywhere within the sheriffdom of Edinburgh."[10] When Arantes gave up and returned to Portugal, Rowling put an even bigger legal obstacle between them: She filed for divorce in August 1994.

It was one of the lowest points in Rowling's life.

Rowling has said that *Harry Potter* saved her:

> *I came back from Portugal to no job and no place to live. I wrote furiously while my daughter was sleeping, which not only gave me something to do with my brain but was an escape for me, too. Corny as it sounds, if the book had never been published it would still have been a hugely important part of my*

life because it gave me some place to go other than a grotty flat in which I felt trapped.[11]

Rowling's life had settled into a routine. Her first priority was the care and nurturing of her daughter. In the afternoons, she would put Jessica into a stroller and wheel her down the main streets of Edinburgh. As soon as Jessica fell asleep, Rowling would stop at Nicholson's Café, a small restaurant owned by her brother-in-law, Roger Moore, and his business partners. Sipping a cup of coffee, Rowling would sit at a table by the window, busy with pen and paper until Jessica woke up. At Nicholson's, she had the company of other people without the intrusion of conversation, and, just as important, she had coffee: "I was in search of good coffee, frankly, and not having to interrupt the flow by getting up and making myself more coffee."[12] Slowly but steadily, as the weeks passed, *Harry Potter* grew from an idea into a handful of chapters. Her story was on its way to becoming a full novel.

By December 1994, Rowling knew she could no longer put off finding a job. She desperately needed more money than public assistance provided, and she also needed to get out of the house more. Being isolated is not good for someone with depression. She had been seeing a therapist to treat her clinical depression for about nine months, and she was ready to make a change in her life.[13]

While Jessica slept in her stroller, Rowling grabbed a few minutes of quiet, sipping coffee and writing her novel in a café.

The first step was to earn a certificate of education so she could teach in the Edinburgh schools. In January 1995 Rowling applied to Heriot-Watt University in Edinburgh for a one-year program. Applicants were subjected to a day-long interview, a written exam, and an interview in the foreign language that they planned to teach. Rowling sought certification in French, which she had studied at Exeter. After going through the extensive application process, Rowling was accepted into the program—an achievement, considering that only one of every four applicants was admitted.[14]

Rowling suffered a brief setback when she discovered that, despite what she had been told, the school no longer provided child care.[15] Then her friend Fiona Wilson, another struggling single mother, stepped in to help. Wilson understood the importance to Rowling of earning the teaching certificate and insisted on lending her money to help pay for child care. Rowling was overwhelmed:

> *I broke down and cried when my friend offered it to me. At the time it was like half a million pounds to me. It was this enormous sum of money. I think we both thought I would never be able to pay it back. The friend was saying, in effect: "Here is a gift to help you."*[16]

Wilson's generosity made it possible for Rowling to go back to school. Classes started in June 1995. The program represented a big step forward for Rowling—a step out of poverty, a step toward independence—but it also complicated her life. For the first time since Jessica's birth, Rowling was away from her child for long periods of time.

> *I found it a terrible wrench to leave my daughter—up until then we had been together 24 hours a day,*

> *and then suddenly we were separated for the vast majority of the day. I found that very difficult. But I did believe it was an investment in her future, so that's really what made me strong enough to do it.*[17]

Rowling was also exhausted from an overwhelming schedule. Her life now consisted of getting up and preparing Jessica for day care, dropping Jessica off at day care, attending classes or student-teaching all day, taking care of Jessica until bedtime, and then spending her last few waking hours working on *Harry Potter*. "I can remember being so tired I would fall asleep on buses. I was writing at the same time as doing the PGCE [postgraduate certification of education]. It tipped me over the edge and took me into zombie territory."[18]

Even so, Rowling did well in the Heriot-Watt program and was an effective and well-liked student teacher. She also continued to work on her novel until, in 1995, she finally completed *Harry Potter and the Philosopher's Stone*.

5 UNEXPECTED FAME

More than five years after the idea had come to her on the train from London, Rowling had finished writing *Harry Potter and the Philosopher's Stone*. The next step was obvious, even if she had no clear idea how to accomplish it: How would she get her book published?

Rowling did not know any published authors who could give her advice. But she did know that she needed a literary agent to present her manuscript to publishers. So she went to Edinburgh's great Central Library, found a reference book titled *Writers' & Artists' Yearbook*, and looked up the names of literary agents. She picked out some names that sounded promising, went home and packed up her manuscript, and sent it out.

Rowling did not have a computer, so she had typed

Harry Potter and the Philosopher's Stone on an old typewriter. Then, because she could not afford to pay for a photocopy, she typed another full copy. One copy was for her; the other was for publishers. She intended to try agent after agent, and publisher after publisher, until someone finally agreed to publish her book.

Rowling placed her first three chapters into a plastic folder (something no experienced author would have done, since the folder made it look more like a high school book report than a professional manuscript), and mailed it out. The first literary agent returned her manuscript with a curt rejection. Immediately, she sent it out again, this time to the Christopher Little Literary Agency.

The Christopher Little Literary Agency was a small agency better known at the time for representing writers of crime fiction. It had no children's authors on its list of clients. Bryony Evens, an assistant at the Christopher Little Literary Agency, was in charge of opening the mail. Every morning, she sorted the incoming manuscripts into two piles: (1) work that the Little Agency handled and (2) work that it did not. *Harry Potter* was placed on the reject pile simply because Christopher Little did not take on children's authors.

The first literary agent returned her manuscript with a curt rejection.

Still, the odd plastic folder holding the pages caught Evens's eye. She loved children's literature, so why not take a peek before returning it to the author with the agency's rejection letter? Evens picked up the folder and flipped through it. Her interest was further heightened by some drawings. Rowling had illustrated some of the pages with her own artwork. Intrigued, Evens sat down and started to read the plot summary and the opening chapters.

Bryony Evens fell in love with *Harry Potter*. She was caught by the story and the characters. Most important, she fell in love with Jo's sense of humor, which flowed through every line. Evens was in the middle of the first chapter when she was interrupted by Fleur Howle, one of the manuscript readers who worked for the agency. It was Howle's job to read author proposals, recommend the good ones, and work with the authors to prepare their work for submission to publishers. At Evens's urging, Howle read the second and third chapters as Evens was finishing the first. Both were eager to see the rest of the manuscript. They asked Christopher Little, owner of the agency, for permission to contact the author.

The agency mailed a short note to Rowling: "Thank you. We would be pleased to receive the balance of your manuscript on an exclusive basis."[1] Rowling later said, "It was far and away the best letter I had ever received in my life, and it was only two sentences long."[2] Rowling made sure they had the rest of the manuscript within the week.

Rowling knew that her book was nearly twice as long as the average children's book, so she had typed the first copy single-spaced, cramming extra lines onto each page. She hoped the agency would not notice the length, but her trick did not work. Rowling was asked to retype the whole manuscript, using double spacing and filling twice as many pages. It did not matter—the readers at the Christopher Little agency loved the book anyway.

Evens was the first person at the agency to read the whole manuscript: "I read it rapidly because it was really good. I read it in a 'I-can't-put-this-down' sort of way."[3] She then passed it on to Christopher Little himself, who sped through it in a single evening. Like Evens, Christopher Little was impressed, and he agreed to be Rowling's literary agent. In early 1996 the agency sent her a contract, and Rowling signed it. She had crossed the first roadblock on her way to becoming a published author.

As exciting as it was for Rowling to have an agent representing her, it did not guarantee that *Harry Potter* would ever reach print. Jo Rowling was still a long way from earning any money from her writing. Finding an agent is just the first step. The Christopher Little Agency would help Rowling prepare the manuscript to best impress a publisher. Then the agency would begin submitting *Harry Potter* to publishing companies until it was accepted—or until they had exhausted all their possibilities. Publishers are flooded with book ideas and new manuscripts every month. They do not have time to read them all. Many will look only at proposals that come in though a professional literary agent.

The Christopher Little Agency sent out the book to a dozen different publishers, all of whom rejected it. Finally, the children's division of Bloomsbury said it would pay £2,000 for an initial printing of five hundred copies of *Harry Potter and the Philosopher's Stone.* Christopher Little asked another book publisher, HarperCollins, if it wanted to offer more money than Bloomsbury, but the editor there was too busy to consider it. So Bloomsbury's offer was accepted. It was August 1996, and *Harry Potter and the Philosopher's Stone* was going to be published. Jo Rowling was overjoyed.

Publishers are flooded with book ideas and new manuscripts every month.

At a luncheon meeting, Barry Cunningham of Bloomsbury, Christopher Little, and Jo Rowling talked about the book. The experienced publisher warned Rowling not to expect to earn a living from the sale of her book. There was no money in children's literature, he said. Being a published author would not mean she could quit her regular job.

Rowling met with her editor at Bloomsbury to discuss her new book.

Cunningham had an opinion about Rowling's name, too. He felt that *Harry Potter* would appeal to boys, but they might be reluctant to read a book written by a woman. Would Rowling be willing to use her initials instead of her full name, Joanne? The three of them considered "J. Rowling" and decided it would sound better with another initial. Rowling picked the letter *K*, for Kathleen, her beloved grandmother. "J. K. Rowling" would be her pen name, the name published on her book.

As Bloomsbury prepared the book for publication, Rowling was completing her teaching certification course. She was also busy writing more about Harry Potter. From the start, she had decided to write seven novels about Harry. Even if they were never published, she still intended to write the whole series of books, if only for herself. In fact, the very day she completed

How Is an Author Paid?

When a publisher decides to publish an author's book, a publishing contract is drawn up by lawyers. Typically, a writer receives some money before the book is published. This is called an "advance," which is short for the phrase "advance against royalties." Once the book hits the bookstores, the author will be paid a royalty—a small amount of money for each book sold. The amount that was paid in advance will later be subtracted from the royalty earnings.

Once book sales exceed the advance amount, the author starts getting royalty checks when more copies are sold. Publishers try to predict how well a book will sell in deciding how much money to give the author as an advance. They do not want to pay more in advance than a book will eventually earn in sales.

Harry Potter and the Philosopher's Stone, she had started working on the second book, *Harry Potter and the Chamber of Secrets.*

Rowling knew that a teaching job and a published book were coming her way, but right now money was still a problem. She could not afford to buy a computer or word processor—yet her system of writing the books out by hand, then typing them on an old-fashioned typewriter, was much too time-consuming. She decided to apply for a grant from the Scottish Arts Council, which gave money to artists. After reviewing her request and her unpublished manuscript, the Scottish Arts Council agreed to give Rowling £8,000 ($13,000) the largest grant it had ever given to a children's author.[4] She used some of the money to buy a word processor to replace her old typewriter. The rest of the money would pay for her living expenses temporarily so that she could finish her second book.

Harry Potter and the Philosopher's Stone was scheduled to arrive in British bookstores on June 26, 1997. Just three days before that, Scholastic, Inc., had paid an astounding amount of money for the right to publish the book in America. The publicity about this deal had a fantastic effect on sales in Great Britain. People were eager to read the book that had set off such a frenzy of bidding. The first printing of *Harry Potter and the Philosopher's Stone* disappeared from bookstores in no time at all, and Bloomsbury found itself printing more books in ever-greater numbers.

While the publicity—and public curiosity—may have increased sales in the beginning, it would not have been enough to sustain interest if children had not wanted to read it. And read it they did. Children were wildly enthusiastic about the book and recommended it to their friends. Children read it, their older brothers and sisters read it—and soon their parents were reading it, too. In the first year of publication in Great Britain, *Harry Potter and the Philosopher's Stone* sold more than seventy thousand copies, an astonishing number for a children's book.[5]

The idea behind the *Harry Potter* story was simple enough. Harry, orphaned when he was a year old, now lives with his aunt Petunia, uncle Vernon, and cousin Dudley. Harry has

Will the Real Harry Potter Please Stand Up?

Many fans and journalists have wondered about the real-life inspirations for the characters in *Harry Potter*. Both Rowling's childhood friend Ian Potter and her cousin Ben Rowling have claimed to be the "real" Harry Potter. Her cousin has even offered to take a lie detector test on American television. Interviewers and biographers have claimed to have evidence that other characters are based on real-life people and that locations in the book were inspired by places where Rowling has lived. Rowling has talked about two of the characters. She says that Professor Gilderoy Lockhart, the Defense Against the Dark Arts instructor in *Harry Potter and the Chamber of Secrets*, is modeled on a real person, though she will not reveal who it is. As for Hermione Granger: "Hermione is the character who is most consciously based on a real person, and that person is me."[6] Beyond that, she says, all her characters are imaginary, although some may occasionally have a quirk shared by a real person in her life.

been treated quite badly by his aunt and uncle for most of his life, sleeping in a closet under the staircase and wearing Dudley's hand-me-down clothing. He was told that his parents were killed in a car crash—an accident that left him with a peculiar scar on his forehead.

On the night of his eleventh birthday, Harry is visited by Rubeus Hagrid, an unkempt giant of a man who reveals the truth: Harry's parents were wizards, and Harry himself is a wizard. Hagrid has come to invite Harry to the wizarding school, Hogwarts School of Witchcraft and Wizardry. Hogwarts follows the typical English school system, in which children spend seven years at school, enrolling at age eleven and graduating at age eighteen.

In his first year at Hogwarts, Harry becomes close friends with Ron Weasley and Hermione Granger, two of the other students living in Gryffindor, one of the four houses at Hogwarts. All the students who live in the same house take classes together, spend time together in the house, and play on the same sports teams. Much of the book is spent describing the experiences they have during their first year—especially their dealings with rivals from another house, Draco Malfoy and his cronies. During the year, Harry learns more about how his parents died at the hands of the evil Lord Voldemort and how Harry managed to survive the attack. Harry, Ron, and Hermione eventually solve a mystery involving Lord Voldemort, showing tremendous courage and quick wit in the process. The book ends at the close of the school year as the students return home for summer vacation.

While the plot of *Harry Potter and the Philosopher's Stone* is clever and original, the key to the extraordinary success of the book is Rowling's writing. In her years of planning Harry Potter's story, Rowling created a vivid, realistic world with hundreds of small details that capture—and keep—her readers' interest. Fans know everything about the food and drink at Hogwarts (chocolate frogs and pumpkin juice), the clothing (Ron's cloak is too small and ragged around the hem), and the games (quidditch, the wizarding sport, with all its rules and details). Readers know the personalities of the various students and learn every character's history. They are entertained by Rowling's dry, tongue-in-cheek humor while being captivated by Harry's plight.

The orphaned Harry Potter is essentially alone in the world and misses his parents terribly. In one scene, Harry pulls out the Mirror of Erised, a magic mirror that reveals the deepest desires of a person's heart. Harry gazes into the eyes of his parents, who wave and smile at him. When his friend Ron looks into the mirror, he admires himself as the head boy of Gryffindor and captain of the quidditch team. Through Rowling's masterful writing, the reader grasps both the heartbreak of Harry's vision and the humor of Ron's.

Many critics have tried to find similarities between Rowling's books and the work of other fantasy writers, such as J.R.R. Tolkien (author of the *Lord of the Rings* trilogy). An equally apt parallel could be drawn between Rowling and Douglas Adams, author of *A Hitchhiker's Guide to the Galaxy*, or between Rowling's humor and that of the English comedy troupe Monte Python.

Readers quickly embraced *Harry Potter and the Philosopher's Stone* and made it a best-selling book. British children were wild enough about Harry to award the book the Smarties Prize for Children's Literature in 1997. It also won the Federation of Children's Book Group Children's Book Award for 1997, the British Book Awards' Children's Book of the Year for 1997, and a Sheffield Children's Book Award in 1998.

In July 1998, about a year after *Harry Potter and the Philosopher's Stone* first appeared in Great Britain, Bloomsbury published Rowling's second book, *Harry Potter and the Chamber of Secrets.* In Harry's second year at Hogwarts, the students are threatened by an unknown monster that is let out of an ancient room hidden deep within the school. As the months pass and the creature continues to attack students, Professor Dumbledore warns that Hogwarts will have to be closed unless the monster can be stopped. Harry, Ron, and Hermione spend the school year solving the mystery of what the monster is, how to find it, and who might have unleashed it on the school.

Harry Potter had already become so popular in Britain that on the day the second book was released, children and parents gathered at bookstores all over the country, anxious to get a copy before the book sold out. The mood was festive, and many bookstores turned the occasion into a party for their customers. Readers came dressed as their favorite *Harry Potter* character. J. K. Rowling was scheduled to give public readings throughout England and Scotland, and found that each event was packed with children and parents. "The very best moment was meeting the mother of a dyslexic nine-year-old, who told me Harry Potter was the first book he'd ever finished all by himself. She said she'd burst into tears when she found him reading it in bed

The Nestlé Smarties Prize

One of the top awards for children's literature in Great Britain is the Nestlé Smarties Book Prize. It was first given in 1984. Books in three different age groups (five and under, six to eight years, and 9 to 11 years) are honored with gold, silver, and bronze awards. Each year a panel of judges selects a list of books, then invites British schoolchildren to vote for their favorites. Rowling would win a Smarties Book Prize gold award for three years in a row: *Harry Potter and the Philosopher's Stone* won for the nine-to-eleven age group in 1997. Her next book, *Harry Potter and the Chamber of Secrets*, would win in 1998; and her third book in the series, *Harry Potter and the Prisoner of Azkaban*, would take the prize in 1999. After three Smarties Prizes, Rowling asked the judges not to consider her books for future competitions. She wanted to be fair and give other authors an opportunity to win.

the morning after she'd read the first two chapters aloud to him. I'm not sure I managed to convey to her what a wonderful thing that was to hear, because I thought I was going to cry too."[7]

The excitement over *Harry Potter* in Great Britain crossed the Atlantic to the United States, even though neither of the books had yet

Rowling gives special attention to every reader she meets.

been published there. As *Harry Potter and the Philosopher's Stone* continued to win awards and rave reviews in Great Britain, American readers became more and more eager to read Harry's adventures for themselves. Finally, in September 1998, Scholastic, Inc., published the first volume of *Harry Potter* in the United States.

The book's instant popularity meant that Rowling was asked to do her first U.S. book tour. In October 1998, she traveled to five different American cities to sign books at various bookstores. Even though *Harry Potter and the Sorcerer's Stone* had a growing number of fans, Rowling herself was still unknown and was treated like any other author. She brought five-year-old Jessica along on tour and was happy to greet readers at every stop. In fact, Rowling said later, one of the highlights of the trip occurred at a bookstore in Seattle, when a woman came in asking if they had *Harry Potter*. The bookstore owner replied that

From Philosopher to Sorcerer

The book that American readers saw was not exactly like the book that British readers had bought months earlier. Scholastic changed the American title to *Harry Potter and the Sorcerer's Stone*, thinking that American readers would be more familiar with the phrase "Sorcerer's Stone" than they would be with "Philosopher's Stone." Inside the book, Scholastic changed a handful of words that have different meanings in England and the United States. "Jumper," for instance, became "sweater," the word used by American readers.

Harry Goes to Hollywood

The astonishing success of *Harry Potter* meant that film studios were eager to turn the books into movies. After Warner Brothers bought the rights to make the movies, studio executives consulted with Rowling to make certain that the films would be made to her satisfaction. From the beginning, Rowling insisted that all the actors in the cast must be British. This caused director Steven Spielberg to lose interest in the project. He had wanted an American actor, Haley Joel Osment, to play Harry.[8] Rowling had some specific casting requests, too. She wanted Robbie Coltrane to play Rubeus Hagrid, and Alan Rickman to play Severeus Snape.

Once the director—Christopher Columbus—was selected for the first film, the search began for the right actors to fill the parts. Columbus personally selected Daniel Radcliffe to play Harry. Daniel had already appeared in two movies, and his natural resemblance to drawings of Harry was obvious to everyone. The actors chosen to play Ron Weasley (Rupert Grint) and Hermione Granger (Emma Watson) were unknowns, selected from hundreds of other young actors at casting calls.

Some of the cast of *Harry Potter,* clockwise from top left: Richard Harris, Robbie Coltrane, Emma Watson, Daniel Radcliffe, and Rupert Grint.

they not only had the book, they had the author—sitting at a table right there. It was a delightful coincidence. The woman had not known that Rowling would be in the store that day.[9]

Rowling's life as a regular, nonfamous person was coming to a close. Authors (even authors of best-selling books) usually are not recognized by fans on the street, or mobbed by people in bookstores—that treatment is reserved for movie stars. And in October 1998, Rowling became one of those rare authors to gain the status of a movie star when Warner Brothers Pictures announced that it had bought the film rights to *Harry Potter* for a large sum of money.

With so many big events happening in so short a period of time—the publication of two best-selling books in Great Britain, a third book already completed and moving along toward publication, a best-selling book in the United States, and an important film deal—Rowling's name and photograph began to appear in newspapers and magazines around the world. *Harry Potter*'s creator was becoming nearly as famous as Harry Potter himself.

For the National Portrait Gallery in London, artist Stuart Pearson Wright portrayed Rowling in a three-dimensional construction in mixed media. She sits alone, writing, at a small table near a window.

6 FAME AND FORTUNE

Rowling spent much of the first half of 1999 working on her fourth book, *Harry Potter and the Goblet of Fire.* Her increasing fame meant that she lost the ability to sit unnoticed in a favorite café for hours at a time, writing and drinking coffee. She was no longer free to write in the way she had written the first two *Harry Potter* volumes:

> *My ideal writing space is a large café with a small corner table near a window overlooking an interesting street (for gazing out of in search of inspiration). It would serve very strong coffee and be non-smoking . . . and nobody would notice me at all. But I can't write in cafés any more because I would get recognized a lot.*[1]

As Rowling became more successful, she received more requests from people and charities for assistance.

She was asked to donate money, her name, and her time to promote a wide variety of causes. One of the most difficult requests that Rowling receives is from parents of terminally ill children who hope that Rowling will reveal the plot of the next unpublished book to them while their child is still alive. Rowling is strict about safeguarding the secrecy of unpublished *Harry Potter* material, but she has been unable to resist trying to comfort these readers and their families.

Many people and charities began asking Rowling for help.

Nine-year-old Natalie McDonald was dying of leukemia in the summer of 1999. She was a devoted fan of *Harry Potter*, and the books became her refuge from illness in the last months of her life. A friend of her family began sending emails to J. K. Rowling's publisher, trying to get in touch with the author. Unfortunately, Rowling was out of town. She had been working very hard on *Harry Potter and the Goblet of Fire* and had decided to take a short vacation in Spain. As soon as she returned home, she tried to reach Natalie, but it was too late. Natalie had died the day before, on August 3, 1999.

Rowling kept in touch with Natalie's mother, Valerie McDonald, and arranged for Valerie, her husband, and their other daughters to visit her in Edinburgh the next year. Rowling also made a special gesture in honor of Natalie's memory. In *Harry Potter and the Goblet of Fire*, the sorting hat would call out "Natalie McDonald" and admit the girl to Gryffindor. Natalie McDonald is one of only two real names used in any of the *Harry Potter* books.[2] (The other is Nicholas Flamel, a real medieval alchemist mentioned in *The Sorcerer's Stone.*)

Rowling's quiet life of writing was interrupted after the second *Harry Potter* book came out in the United States. After reading the first book, American readers had become too impatient to wait another year for the Scholastic edition of *Harry Potter and the Chamber of Secrets.* So they had started ordering it directly from England. A few bookstores tried to import the English version to sell here, until they learned that doing so was against the law. The American publisher Scholastic owned the exclusive right to sell *Harry Potter* in the United States. To meet the growing demand from American readers, Scholastic had finally taken the unheard-of step of releasing *Harry Potter and the Chamber of Secrets* on June 2, 1999, three months earlier than first planned. Rowling's second book, too, was an immediate bestseller in the United States.

American readers did not want to wait a year for Rowling's next book.

After that, there would be no more time lags

between the British and American editions of Rowling's books. The third book in the series, *Harry Potter and the Prisoner of Azkaban*, was published on September 8, 1999, in both Great Britain and the United States. For this book, Rowling's publishers insisted that all bookstores start selling the book at exactly the same time on exactly the same date. That way, no one would be able to get an early copy and ruin the plot for other readers.

Harry's third year at Hogwarts starts badly. In an argument with his uncle's sister, he loses his temper and causes her to float into the air and go sailing off over London. Harry runs away from his uncle's house to the Leaky Cauldron, where he discovers the Ministry of Magic has no intention of punishing him as he had expected. He soon discovers that everyone is concerned about him because they believe that a recently escaped prisoner from Azkaban, the wizard's prison, is trying to find Harry to murder him on behalf of Lord Voldemort. Harry spends the year learning about the background of the prisoner, Sirius Black, and what actually happened when his parents were murdered.

The reaction to *The Prisoner of Azkaban* was as enthusiastic as it had been to *Chamber of Secrets*: Children crowded into bookstores, wildly cheering for Rowling, and bought the book by the thousands. It immediately made the *New York Times* best-seller list.

Rowling discovered on her book tour for *The*

Crowds gathered outside a Chicago bookstore in October 1999 as fans waited for a turn to meet Rowling.

Prisoner of Azkaban that her fame and popularity made the trip overwhelming for both the author and her readers. With at least a thousand fans swarming every store, her publisher put a limit on the number of books Rowling could sign at each sitting. "It's amazing—it's like traveling with a rock star," said the publisher's representative.[3] Bookstores had to hire extra security and give out tickets for readers to meet the author. Even so, not every store visit went well. At a book signing in Livingston, New Jersey, the swarm of more than two thousand became impossible to control. Some people pushed their way to the front of the lines, and many children were turned away from the store. At one point, the crowd became so ugly that the store manager was bitten and punched.[4]

By the end of her three-week U.S. tour, Rowling had signed more than forty thousand books at thirty-one different stores.[5] As exhausting as this must have been for Rowling, she gave each reader personal attention. Steve Geck, a Barnes & Noble representative, was impressed:

> *She thanked each and every one of them for reading her books and for coming to meet her. If she met a boy wearing glasses, she'd remark that he looked a bit like Harry. She made everyone feel so good—people just floated away from the table.*[6]

The October 1999 book tour also marked the first time that large numbers of readers appeared at book signings in specially made *Harry Potter* costumes, instead of general witch and wizard clothing. Children dressed up as Harry, Ron, Hermione, and even Hedwig the owl. Many bookstores were concerned about keeping fans entertained while they stood in such long lines, so they hired magicians or organized readings from the *Harry Potter* books. This led to the creation of *Harry Potter* publication parties, with bookstores staging elaborate events on the publication date of the latest *Harry Potter* book.

With the publication of *Harry Potter and the Prisoner of Azkaban*, Rowling's financial worries were over. The most obvious impact of the wild success of

This Dallas, Texas, bookstore set up a magic show to entertain eager fans.

Harry Potter on Rowling's life was financial: In a very short period of time, she went from poverty to wealth. "I never expected to make money," she has said. "I always saw Harry Potter as this quirky little book. I liked it and I worked hard at it, but never in my wildest dreams did I imagine large advances."[7]

Throughout the first months of 2000 Rowling continued to work on *Harry Potter and the Goblet of Fire.* Her writing was going smoothly, until one day early in 2000 a friend warned her that her ex-husband, Jorge Arantes, had sold his story to a British tabloid newspaper. When Rowling found and read the interview, she was horrified to discover what had been written. Even worse was the fact that photographs of her daughter Jessica had been published. Rowling was particularly upset by the photographs because she had worked very hard to protect her daughter from the fame that the *Harry Potter* books had brought to them. She sat down to continue her work on *Harry Potter and the Goblet of Fire*, but she realized that she was much too disturbed by the tabloid story to be able to write a word. To shake off this mood and her temporary writer's block, she decided to do something very unusual: She was going to go out and buy a gift for herself. Although Rowling now had enough money from *Harry Potter* to create a comfortable life for herself and Jessica, she rarely bought anything extravagant:

> *I didn't immediately become very rich. The biggest jump for me was the American advance, which was enough for me to buy a house, not outright, but you know we'd been renting until then. And I didn't feel guilty, I felt scared at that point. Because I thought I mustn't blow this: I've got some money, I mustn't do anything stupid with it. And then yeah, yeah, I felt guilty.*[8]

But this was a special occasion, because it interfered with her ability to work on her book. She decided to visit a jeweler and buy herself a ring—a very large

"I never expected to make money," said Rowling, who has become one of the richest women in the world.

aquamarine ring. She purchased it impulsively and occasionally calls it the "No One Is Grinding Me Down" ring.[9]

> *I love [the ring], and I also love it because of what it represents to me, what it actually represents to me is how I got over a very, very bad day, I'd had a very bad week, when I went out and bought that ring. I was . . . you know, when people start searching your [trash] bins, as has literally happened to me, it's horrible. It feels like such an invasion, and I'm not a politician, I'm not an entertainer, I never expected that level of interest in my life, and it feels so invasive. And I was having a very bad day, thinking, What have I done to deserve this? What have I done?*[10]

Apparently being able to buy herself a gift helped. Her writer's block lifted, and Rowling went back to work on *Harry Potter and the Goblet of Fire.*

She had one little reader who was particularly impatient for *The Goblet of Fire.* One of the millions of fans of *The Prisoner of Azkaban* was a nine-year-old girl named Catie Hoch. She was ill with a very rare form of childhood cancer. The *Harry Potter* books gave her tremendous pleasure. In fact, when she took the train from Albany to New York City for medical treatments, she dressed as Harry Potter. Catie and her parents continued to read the books throughout her illness. They

What would happen in the fourth book? Rowling told some secrets to a dying child.

were nearing the end of *Harry Potter and the Prisoner of Azkaban* when doctors told Catie's parents that she would not live much longer. Catie's wish was to read the fourth book of the series, *Harry Potter and the Goblet of Fire*, but Rowling had not yet finished writing the book.

A friend of the family told Rowling about Catie's situation, and Rowling sent Catie an email. They began to correspond regularly, with Catie dictating her answers to her mother. Rowling sent Catie gifts for Valentine's Day and for her birthday. Finally, when it was clear that Catie's death was near, her mother wrote to Rowling and told her so. Rowling called the Hoch home and asked if she could read portions of the unpublished *Goblet of Fire* to Catie over the phone. The family made Catie comfortable on the sofa, and Rowling read to her. She called Catie a few more times and read more of *Goblet of Fire* to her, until Catie was at last too ill to take her phone calls.[11] Catie died in May 2000.

Harry Potter and the Goblet of Fire was published in Britain and the United States on July 8, 2000. This was the longest book yet, more than twice as long as *The Prisoner of Azkaban.* Harry Potter fans were not put off by the size of the book, and many children found themselves reading all night to find out what happened.

The beginning of Harry's fourth year at Hogwarts finds him joining the Weasley family and Hermione Granger for a trip to the quidditch World Cup match. When the match is over and the students return to Hogwarts, they learn that there will be no quidditch matches held at school this year. Instead, a rare contest called the Triwizard Tournament will be

Making Room for Adult Books

Every *Harry Potter* has made the best-seller lists and has stayed there for months. After Rowling's books had taken the top three spots on the *New York Times* best-seller list for more than a year, the newspaper decided to make two lists—one for adult books, and one for children's books. Rowling's fourth book was about to be released, and other publishers and authors were beginning to complain that the presence of three, and possibly four, *Harry Potter* books on the best-seller list made it impossible for them to earn a place.

held on the Hogwarts grounds. Students from the wizarding schools of Beauxbatons and Durmstrangs will be spending the year at Hogwarts, and one student aged eighteen or older from each school will compete in the tournament. Everyone is shocked when the Goblet of Fire selects not three students but four. One of them is Harry Potter, who is only fourteen years old.

Rowling's book tour in England included a ride on the antique steam train that appears in the *Harry Potter* films as the Hogwarts Express. Although the publishers expected the train trip to be a joyful and festive event—the train was scheduled to stop at certain stations so that Rowling could meet her fans—it actually turned out to be somewhat unpleasant. Rowling was forced to travel with private security guards because of letters she had been receiving from a stalker; even though the man had not threatened her, his obsessive letters made her publishers fear for Rowling's safety. The crowds at each train station were so huge that hundreds of children were disappointed that they were unable to meet Rowling. At one station, a father tried to push through the crowd with his young daughter. He knocked over a photographer, and an angry argument erupted between them. His daughter was left sobbing.[12]

Less than a week after *The Goblet of Fire* was published, Rowling returned to the University of Exeter to receive an honorary doctorate for her success

Rowling leaned out the window of the "Hogwarts Express" train to greet her fans.

with *Harry Potter*. At the ceremony, the professor who introduced her to the audience joked about the advice that had been given to Rowling by her agent Christopher Little before the publication of her first book: "Now remember, Joanne, this is all very well, but it is not going to make your fortune."[13]

But *Harry Potter* was making Rowling's fortune. She was responding to her sudden wealth by making donations to charities and social causes about which she was passionate. In October 2000, she agreed to become spokesperson for the National Council for One Parent Families, when Andy Downs, the director, knocked on her door.

> *"Andy," I interrupted, in that harassed voice by which lone parents can often be identified, "you'd like me to be Patron, wouldn't you?" "Well, we're calling it Ambassador," said Andy. . . . "OK, I'll do it," I said, "but could we please discuss the details on the way to school, because Sports Day starts in five minutes." And so we discussed the National Council for One Parent Families while watching the egg-and-spoon races; a fitting start, I felt, for my association with a charity devoted to helping those parents whose lives are a constant balancing act.*[14]

Although she was now a famous and wealthy author, she remembered very clearly what it was like to

Rowling is glad she can use her fame and fortune to help others. Here, she spoke about the National Council for One Parent Families.

be an impoverished single parent. She remembered the depression and exhaustion she had felt as she tried to care for her daughter, get her teaching certificate, and write in what little spare time was left. Rowling was determined to help other single parents in whatever way she could. Not only did she agree to serve as spokesperson, she donated £500,000 to the National Council of One Parent Families.

In December 2000, Rowling was invited to Buckingham Palace in England for an honor awarded to very few British subjects. In a special ceremony, Queen Elizabeth herself planned to welcome Rowling as an officer of the Order of the British Empire for her contributions to children's literature. When Rowling's seven-year-old daughter, Jessica, became ill, Rowling did not want to leave her.[15]

The ceremony was rescheduled, and Rowling traveled from Edinburgh to receive her OBE (Order of the British Empire) from Prince Charles on March 2, 2001.[16] Rowling met Queen Elizabeth a few weeks later, when the queen came to Bloomsbury's offices on a visit promoting Britain's publishing industry.[17]

Rowling and her publishers had decided not to publish a *Harry Potter* book in 2001. At least one new book had been published each year since the first book appeared in 1997, and everyone felt that Rowling should be able to take a break and write the fifth book at a slower, more comfortable pace. While Rowling

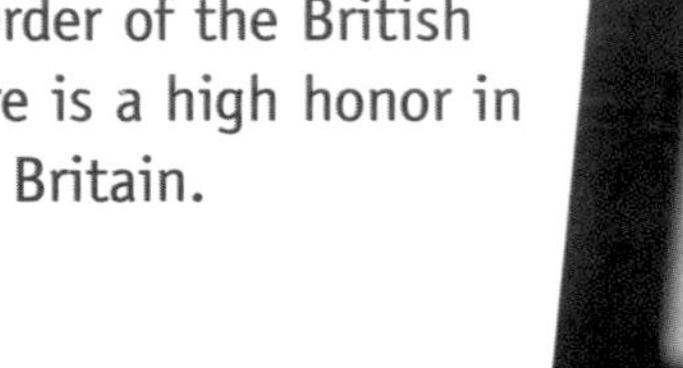

The Order of the British Empire is a high honor in Great Britain.

Fame also brought Rowling honorary college degrees, like this one from Edinburgh's Napier University in 2001.

worked on *Harry Potter and the Order of the Phoenix*, she found more time to give to charities. Having already donated a great deal of money and time to the National Council for One Parent Families, Rowling now made an equal commitment to the Multiple Sclerosis Society of Scotland.

The death of Anne Rowling from multiple sclerosis at age forty-five had been very traumatic for Jo. Her fame and wealth now enabled her to translate her grief for her mother into positive action.

> *For me, being able to campaign and fund-raise for multiple sclerosis is the most personally meaningful thing to have come out of being famous. It would mean everything to me if I thought even one person did not have to go through what my mother did.*[18]

Rowling became a patron—a major supporter—of the Multiple Sclerosis Society of Scotland in April 2001. She does more than simply lend her name to the organization. She is an active fund-raiser, hoping that more money for research will lead to better treatment, if not a cure. She also donates her own funds, and she writes articles about her mother for the official publication of the MS Society.

Rowling also made a commitment to Britain's Comic Relief, a group established by comedians and entertainers to raise money to fight poverty, disease, and social problems around the world. Rowling learned about Comic Relief from Richard Curtis, a screenwriter who created the *Bridget Jones* movies. Curtis asked Rowling if she would consider donating something for an auction, with the proceeds going to Comic Relief's projects. He hoped that she might autograph a Harry Potter novel for them, or perhaps even write a short article for them.

Rowling stunned Curtis by offering to write two books for the group, with all proceeds from the sale of the books to be given to Comic Relief. She told Curtis that she had dozens of ideas left over from writing *Harry Potter*, but could not find an appropriate place to put them into that series. The books she gave to Comic Relief are *Quidditch Through the Ages: The Definitive History of the Wizard's Favorite Three-Dimensional Flying Game* and *Fantastic Beasts and Where to Find Them.*[19] They were published in 2001, and in their first six months in print, the two books raised nearly $1.4 million for Comic Relief.[20]

There are other isolated acts of extraordinary generosity as well. In the summer of 2001 Rowling repaid her old friend Fiona Wilson, who had lent her £4,000 for child care while she earned her teaching certificate. Rowling gave Wilson the home she owned in the Merchiston neighborhood of Edinburgh. She had bought the home with the first advance she received for *Harry Potter*. Now that she had even more money, she had purchased another home in a different part of the city.[21] It meant more to Rowling to give the home to her friend than to sell it and take the profit.

The summer of 2001 was significant for Rowling not just because of her increased charity work. Her relationship with Neil Murray, a young doctor just finishing his training, was becoming public. Rowling had always told the press that her life was full and satisfying with Jessica and with her writing. Of course it would be nice to fall in love again, and she had hoped to have more children one day, but she knew that relationships were not easy for people in the public eye. It might be increasingly difficult to meet someone who valued her as an individual, not as the creator of Harry Potter. But Murray seemed unaware of Rowling's fame, or what it might mean:

> *The night we met he told me he had read the first ten pages of* Philosopher's Stone *on a late-night shift at the hospital and he thought it was quite good. And I thought that was fantastic. He hadn't read the books. He didn't really have a very clear idea of who I was. It meant that we could get to know each other in quite a normal way. I think he's up to speed now, poor bloke. At the time he didn't really have any idea about it all.*[22]

Because Rowling was now a celebrity, it did not take long for the press to learn that she was dating

J. K. Rowling and Neil Murray

someone, and to pursue them whenever possible. Rowling and Murray were able to keep their relationship very private until they took a vacation on Mauritius, an island off the coast of Africa, in the summer of 2001. Rumors began to fly around the world that the two had eloped, and that a private wedding had been held. Rowling tried to deny these rumors, and finally in October 2001 issued an official press release: "And while we are on the subject of non-news, some people seem to need reminding that wearing a swimsuit in the vicinity of a man in shorts does not constitute a marriage ceremony, even on Mauritius."[23]

The film version of *Harry Potter and the Sorcerer's Stone* opened on November 18, 2001. Despite so-so reviews from many film critics, the movie became an instant success. It opened in more theaters than any other film and boosted *Harry Potter*'s popularity to new heights.

The success of the movie was not the highlight of the year for Rowling, however. A much more private event was quietly announced to the press at the end of the year: Rowling married Neil Murray on December 26, 2001, in their home in Perth, Scotland. Her daughter, Jessica; her sister, Dianne; and Murray's sister Lorna served as bridesmaids.

7 THE WORK CONTINUES

The year 2002 saw the creation of a new family and a new life for Rowling. As she continued to work on *Harry Potter and the Order of the Phoenix*, she also attempted to restore some sense of privacy to her life after the prior year or two of attention from the press.

Unfortunately, Rowling began to experience some of the other common problems that come with sudden fame: stalkers and lawsuits. Stalking occurs when a fan becomes overly attached to a celebrity. There is nothing strange or wrong with writing fan letters to a celebrity. Some fans may drive by a celebrity's home, just to see where the person lives. Stalking is different—and can be dangerous. A stalker often tries to become part of the celebrity's life and family. Stalkers have been known to break into the homes of celebrities, to steal their personal belongings, and to telephone or send mail or email obsessively. This can be a frightening experience. Many stalkers suffer from some type of mental illness, so their behavior is unpredictable, and they may even become violent.

Rowling had become the obsession of an adult American stalker during 2001 and 2002. The thirty-one-year-old woman had moved to Edinburgh and bombarded Rowling with letters and telephone calls. She also started showing up at Rowling's house in Edinburgh and at any public place where she thought Rowling might be present. The woman was arrested in June 2002 and was deported to the United States in July 2002.[1] A month later, Rowling applied for a permit from the Edinburgh City Council to increase the height of the walls surrounding her house and to install an electronic security system. Her neighbors fought her application. They believed that the higher walls and security lights would hurt the beauty of their neighborhood. But the Edinburgh City Council allowed Rowling to increase the security at her home.[2]

Stalking occurs when a fan becomes overly attached to a celebrity.

Lawsuits are another common side effect of fame and fortune. In 2002 Rowling and her publishers were sued for copyright infringement by Nancy Stouffer, author of a children's book titled *The Legend of Rah and the Muggles.* Copyright infringement is the legal term for plagiarism—that is, using someone else's writing without permission. Stouffer also said she had written a book called *Larry Potter and his Best Friend Lilly.* Stouffer claimed that her work was the basis of Rowling's Harry Potter. To win her lawsuit, Stouffer would have needed to convince a court that she was right, and that Rowling had committed copyright infringement. If she won, Stouffer could have taken all of Rowling's profits from *Harry Potter* and could have stopped the publication of any more *Harry Potter* books. None of that happened, because in reality there is no similarity in plot or in the characters, and *Larry Potter* is a simple coloring book.

Banning Books

There has also been a continuing backlash to the popularity of Harry Potter. Fundamentalist Christian groups in the United States and Great Britain have complained that the books promote witchcraft and satanism. Just as the books have continued to be listed on best-seller lists for months on end, they appear on the American Library Association's list of Ten Most Challenged Books year after year. Books are challenged when a librarian receives a written complaint or a request that a book be removed from the library's shelf. Some evangelical churches have gone so far as to burn copies of Harry Potter books for being anti-Christian or sacrilegious.[3] The Catholic Church, on the other hand, has signaled its approval of Harry Potter. A Vatican representative said that the books "help children to see the difference between good and evil" and said that Rowling is "Christian by conviction, is Christian in her mode of living, even in her way of writing."[4]

Fame has its drawbacks, too. Nancy Stouffer's lawsuit claiming Rowling had stolen her creation turned out to be without any merit.

In September 2002 the New York court threw Stouffer's case out of court. The judge ruled that Rowling had not committed copyright infringement of any kind. He also stated that Stouffer had created false evidence to make her claims look better than they were. Stouffer's lawsuit was dismissed "with prejudice" (meaning her lawyers could not file it again), and the judge ordered Stouffer to give Rowling and her attorneys $50,000 to pay for their costs in having to defend the false claim in court.[5]

Rowling has been involved in other lawsuits as well, but these were of a different sort: They have all been filed by Rowling to protect *Harry Potter* from being used illegally by other writers. Because *Harry Potter* is one of the most profitable children's books ever published, authors in other countries have tried to capture some of Rowling's success—either by writing a book just like *Harry Potter*, or by using the *Harry Potter* characters in their own books. Following are some of the more newsworthy examples of Rowling's struggles to protect Harry Potter:

- *Tanya Grotter*, a story of an eleven-year-old Russian witch, was published in Russia as "a Russian reply to *Harry Potter*."[6] It became hugely successful. Rowling sued a Dutch importer in Holland to prevent the book from being imported into Holland on the grounds that the book copied *Harry Potter*. The Dutch court agreed, blocking publication in Holland.

Knockoffs of *Harry Potter* appear around the world. Lawyers put a stop to *Tanya Grotter and the Magical Double Bass*.

- In China, where international copyright law is not often enforced, publishing houses put out illegal versions of all of the real *Harry Potter* books. They also produced additional books written by unidentified Chinese authors and claimed they were written by Rowling. The titles were *Harry Potter and the Leopard-Walk-Up-to-Dragon* (in which Harry is joined by Gandalf, the wizard from *Lord of the Rings*), *Harry Potter and the Golden Turtle*, and *Harry Potter and the Crystal Vase*. Rowling's lawyers had a greater challenge in protecting Harry Potter in China. But they were finally able to obtain an apology from one publishing house and an agreement not to publish any more fake *Harry Potter* books.[7]

- In India, a publishing house produced *Harry Potter in Calcutta*. The book was withdrawn from publication as soon as Rowling's lawyers sent a letter of protest.[8]

- The United States Army used *Harry Potter* look-alike characters in a series of cartoon strips in its publication *Preventive Maintenance Monthly*, distributed to eighty thousand members of the armed forces. Army representatives created characters called Professor Rumble-Doore, Professor Snappy, and Professor Mcdonagal. The cartoon strips showed these characters teaching a Sergeant Half-Mast at Mogmarts School of Magical PM how to take care of his army equipment.[9]

In spite of the frustration and distraction of dealing with stalkers and lawsuits, Rowling managed to continue writing *The Order of the Phoenix*, and to keep up her substantial contributions to charity work.

She hosted a Halloween Ball in 2002, hoping to raise £100,000 for the MS Society. With her help, the event brought in £275,000. Rowling noted, "I can't tell you how happy that made me; I was still beaming about it at the film premiere two days later. We got enough money on that one night to double the number of MS nurses in Scotland."[10] And to honor Catie Hoch, the little girl who died of cancer in 2000, Rowling contributed $100,000 to a fund established by Catie's parents.[11]

Even though no *Harry Potter* book was released in 2002, the public's appetite for the young wizard was satisfied by the release of the second movie. On November 15, 2002, *Harry Potter and the Chamber of Secrets* opened to huge crowds. The movie received slightly better reviews than the first film did, and theaters were packed with *Harry Potter* fans.

Except for occasional appearances at charity events, and very rare interviews in the press—Rowling had cut back drastically on the number of interviews she gave—Rowling managed to live a very private life for most of the year. Her fans did not know it at the time, but part of Rowling's desire for privacy was the fact that she was expecting another child. Her son,

David Gordon Rowling Murray, was born on March 23, 2003.

Rowling did not let her pregnancy and the birth of her son take her completely away from *Harry Potter.* After much anticipation by fans, *Harry Potter and the Order of the Phoenix* was released on June 21, 2003. While many people had speculated that Rowling must have had writer's block—there had never been so long a wait for a *Harry Potter* book before—she denied that this was ever a problem. "I wanted to know what it was like to write without having the pressure of the deadline. And it was wonderful. I had been writing very intensely, since *Philosopher's Stone.* By *Goblet* I was writing 10 hours a day. And that's just getting stupid."[12]

Harry Potter and the Order of the Phoenix was as lengthy a book as *Goblet of Fire*—much longer than typical children's books. Once again fans found themselves reading through the night, eager to get to the end of the story. *Order of the Phoenix* was a much more serious, more adult book than the previous *Harry Potter* volumes. Harry was now fifteen, and his maturity was evident in Rowling's writing. Some readers and critics were surprised by the increasing complexity of the story and of

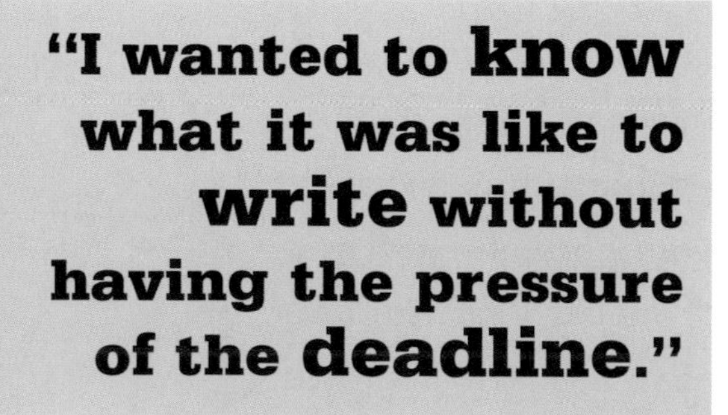

Once again fans found themselves reading through the night, eager to get to the end of the story.

Harry Potter's character, but most fans loved the fact that Rowling was allowing Harry to grow up.

Rowling did not want to take time away from her infant son to do a book tour, so there were no trips to bookstores and libraries as there had been in the past. Rowling did manage to get to one bookstore—Waterstone's, a shop near her home in Edinburgh. Like thousands of bookstores around the world, Waterstone's had organized a *Harry Potter* party to celebrate the release of *Order of the Phoenix* at the stroke of midnight on June 23, 2003. As the clock was striking twelve, the door opened and Rowling walked in. The store manager described the reaction of the children: "It was truly incredible. They saw J.K. coming in and ran towards her. They gathered round her, leaping into the air. They were going bananas. It was magical."[13]

Rather than trying to travel from bookstore to bookstore to meet fans, Rowling has taken to using Webcasts to reach her readers. On June 26, 2003, she was interviewed by the actor Stephen Fry (who reads *Harry Potter* for British audiobooks) in a Webcast at the Royal Albert Hall in London to promote the publication of *Harry Potter and the Order of the Phoenix.*

When her fifth book—*Harry Potter and the Order of the Phoenix*—was released, Rowling made a rare and special appearance at this bookstore in Edinburgh.

They sat on a stage decorated to look like a Hogwarts common room, and behind them were large screens for video questions from fans around the world. Hundreds of children and parents filled the audience. During the course of the interview, questions were taken on video over the Internet (the questions were printed on the screens onstage), and from preselected children in the audience.

While the Webcast meant that Rowling could not enjoy the spontaneity of meeting individual children and their parents, it also prevented the sorts of problems that had occurred in the past. There were no shoving crowds or shouting matches. No children ended up in tears. Best of all, it meant that any child with access to a computer could take part in the Webcast and see Rowling interviewed as it happened.

Any child with access to a computer could take part in the Webcast and see Rowling interviewed.

Rowling continued doing charity work. In 2003 she hosted another gala for the MS Society of Scotland. This time she auctioned off a moment of fame: Two bidders would each get a role as an "extra" in the film version of *Harry Potter and the Goblet of Fire.* An extra is someone who appears in the background of a scene. She also donated a signed leather edition of *Harry Potter and the Order of the Phoenix* to be sold at the auction.

In 2003, Rowling donated £200,000 to villagers in Perth to buy eleven hundred acres of land near Rowling's country home. The land had been run as a deer park (a place where hunters could try to track deer) until the owner decided to sell the property. The local residents wanted to buy the land for conservation. They hoped to return the land to its natural state. "[Rowling] was our knight in shining armour, our very own wizard," said the leader of the community group.[14]

In October 2003, Rowling was awarded the prestigious Prince of Asturias Concord Prize in Spain. She was given the honor "for having helped children of all races and cultures to discover the joy of reading."[15]

As Rowling reclaimed her private life and wrote the next *Harry Potter* installment at a slower pace, it gave her more time to pursue other interests. Partly because she had become interested in the Internet, and partly because she wanted to have better control over rumors about *Harry Potter* (or about herself and her family), she opened her own Web site in May 2004. Now Rowling has a place where she can make official announcements about what will (or will not) happen in an upcoming book, or to deny untrue rumors about something she is said to be doing, or to warn fans about attempted sales of fake *Harry Potter* merchandise (including books with false Rowling autographs being offered on eBay).

Her interest in the Internet also led her to yet another challenge in protecting *Harry Potter:* fan fiction. *Harry Potter*'s great success has made it one of the most popular sources of inspiration for writers of fan fiction. While fan fiction can be flattering to an author, it can also endanger the author's work by allowing characters to be changed and possibly pictured in unflattering ways. Harry Potter is a very good boy and an immensely likable character, and Rowling has a deep emotional attachment to her creation. She does not want amateur writers making up their own stories about Harry and possibly changing the essence of his character.

So far Rowling has met this challenge by leaving some fan-fiction Web sites alone, while instructing her lawyers to send letters to others. She is unwilling to ignore any fan fiction that features *Harry Potter* characters

Fan Fiction

Thanks to the ease of publishing on the Internet, the genre of "fan fiction" has become extremely popular. A fan of a particular work (such as a *Harry Potter* book or *Lord of the Rings*) will write a short story, or even a novel, using characters and settings from the original work. Fan fiction uses another author's work as its setting, so technically it is copyright infringement. It is considered "derivative work"—that is, a work adapted or created from another work. Before publishing fan fiction, on paper or on the Internet, the writer must obtain permission from the author of the original work. Otherwise, as a derivative work, it is illegal.

If the fan fiction is not harming the original work, an author may decide not to take action against it. Derivative works are usually written by people who loved the original—and authors do not want to offend their fans.

By September 2005, the first three *Potter* films had grossed more than $2.5 billion.[16] Movie viewers have watched, from left, Daniel Radcliffe, Emma Watson, and Rupert Grint grow up along with Harry Potter.

in inappropriate situations, particularly those involving violence or sexuality. Rowling's books are written for children, and she believes that any stories that put Harry or his friends in adult situations are contrary to the spirit of her work and, if widely read, would hurt Harry's reputation among readers.[17] She will not allow that to happen.

While no new *Harry Potter* book was published in 2004, the public's love of Hogwarts was satisfied by the release of the third movie, *Harry Potter and the Prisoner of Azkaban.* It opened on June 4, 2004, receiving the best reviews of any of the movies, and earning more money on opening weekend than the first two movies. The original director, Chris Columbus, left the project after the second movie and was replaced by a Mexican director, Alfonso Cuaron.

More important to Rowling than the opening of *Harry Potter and the Prisoner of Azkaban* was the fact that she was expecting her third child. Once again, she and her husband kept the news private for as long as possible.

In spite of being pregnant, taking care of a toddler and a preteen, and continuing to work on *Harry Potter and the Half-Blood Prince,* Rowling managed to keep up her charity work. In November 2004, after years of serving as spokesperson for the National Council of One Parent Families, she agreed to become the president of the organization.[18]

Harry Potter fever has spread around the world, including (1) China, (2) Mexico, (3) Germany, and (4) Switzerland.

The *Harry Potter* books have been translated into more than sixty languages, including Korean, Afrikaans, Turkish, and Estonian—languages from every continent on earth.

That month Rowling was also asked to help with another charity event. It was being held by *Tatler* magazine to benefit an organization helping the homeless. The group sent twenty-four miniature leather-bound books to celebrities. The books were just one inch high, and all the pages were blank. The celebrities were asked to fill the pages of the books, which would be sold at a charity auction. Rowling covered the pages of her tiny book with drawings of Harry's hat, his broomstick, and his wire-rimmed glasses. It was one of the best-selling books at the auction, bringing in £11,000.[19] All the money went to charity.

As Rowling worked to finish *Harry Potter and the Half-Blood Prince*, her daughter Mackenzie Jean Rowling Murray was born on January 23, 2005. When she announced the birth of her daughter, she also reassured fans that Mackenzie would not in any way delay the publication of the sixth *Harry Potter* book.

Perhaps the most important way in which Rowling has repaid the public for its appreciation of her work is by promoting literacy—the ability to read and write. In newspaper and magazine articles, Rowling is often credited with making reading popular again with children. The *Harry Potter* books are successful because children love them, and they share their excitement with their friends.

Rowling is often credited with making reading popular again with children.

No amount of marketing could sell as many books as Rowling has sold. Only first-rate storytelling can accomplish that. Besides writing books that millions of children want to read, Rowling supports literacy by donating money to community centers that promote reading for children. On January 23, 2005, the day her daughter Mackenzie was born, Rowling gave £20,000 to help build and open the Scottish Centre for the Children's Book.[20]

Harry Potter and the Half-Blood Prince was released on July 15, 2005.

Rowling read from *Harry Potter and the Half Blood Prince* in Edinburgh Castle. The youngsters in the audience won contests to write about the book for their local papers.

Rowling's promotional appearance was held in the Great Hall at Edinburgh Castle. She appeared at midnight to read to a group of seventy children who had won competitions held by dozens of English-speaking newspapers.[21] Each child was given a copy of *Harry Potter and the Half-Blood Prince* by Rowling. They had the weekend to read the book in the reading room of Edinburgh Castle, and then met again with Rowling on July 17 to ask questions. Rowling included in the group the creators of the two most popular Harry Potter fan sites, The Leaky Cauldron (http://www.the-leaky-cauldron.org) and Mugglenet (http://www.mugglenet.com). These Webmasters then put detailed reports of the event on their Web sites, so that readers throughout the world could share the experience.

This arrangement gave Rowling the satisfaction of meeting readers face-to-face without the problems of dealing with huge crowds at individual bookstores. When her publisher first suggested it, Rowling responded enthusiastically: "I loved the idea; there is nothing quite as satisfying as sitting in a room with readers whose faces you can see, answering direct questions about your method of writing, characters, and plots."[22]

What's next on the horizon for this amazing author?

8 When Harry Leaves Hogwarts

Harry Potter has been a major part of Rowling's life since he first stepped into her imagination in 1990. What will she do when she finishes the seventh book of the series? What will happen after Harry graduates from Hogwarts?

Rowling has been asked by dozens of readers if there will ever be an eighth book. Will Rowling write about Harry's life after school? Will she write a prequel, telling the story of Harry's parents, James and Lily Potter?

She insists that there will never be a book about James and Lily Potter. She explains that by the time readers have finished the seventh and final book, they will know everything they want to know about Harry's parents.[1] As for writing an eighth book, Rowling's reply is a bit less certain. Harry has been a constant presence in most of her adult life. She has said:

> *The only reason you'll ever see an eighth Harry Potter book is if I really in ten years time, burn to do another one, but at the moment I think that's unlikely. But I try never to say 'never anything,' because at the moment if I say 'I will never,' I do it next month! . . . I just think we're going to stop at seven.*[2]

On the other hand, she admits, finishing Harry's story will leave a huge hole in her life, and that will be difficult to deal with.[3]

Summing up the overall effect *Harry Potter* has had on her life, Rowling has said: "[Writing these books] has made me happier. Finishing them has made me happier. Before I wrote the Potter books, I'd never finished a novel. I came close to finishing two. It also makes me happy that the one thing I thought I could do, I wasn't deluded."[4]

Rowling knows that whatever happens, she will continue to write. She has been writing since she was six years old. Writing is as natural and as necessary to her as breathing. As for what she will write, or what will become of it, she says:

> *I know I will definitely still be writing. Will I publish? I don't know. . . . of course you write to be published, because you write to share the story. But I do think back to what happened to AA Milne*

> [*author of* Winnie the Pooh], *and he of course tried to write adult novels, and was never reviewed without the mention of Tigger, Pooh and Piglet. And I would imagine that the same will happen with me. And that's fine. God knows my shoulders are broad enough, I could cope with that. But I would like some time to have some normal life at the end of the series, and probably the best way to get that isn't to publish immediately.*[5]

It is not hard to imagine that, with her youth and success, Rowling will publish again. Yet, with two very young children and a daughter entering her teens—and with her deep devotion to charity work such as the MS Society—she may choose to retreat into a more private life, concentrating on family and volunteer work. The joy for Rowling is that *Harry Potter* has given her complete freedom to do with her life as she sees fit.

Chronology

1965 Joanne (Jo) Rowling born on July 31 in Yate, England.

1967 Sister, Dianne, is born. Family moves from Yate to Winterbourne.

1974 Family moves from Winterbourne to Tutshill.

1980 Mother, Anne Rowling, is diagnosed with multiple sclerosis (MS).

1983 Jo Rowling enrolls at Exeter University.

1985 Moves to Paris to spend her third year abroad.

1987 Graduates from Exeter University with a degree in French.

1990 Gets the idea for *Harry Potter* on a train trip between London and Manchester. Anne Rowling dies of multiple sclerosis on December 30.

1991 Jo Rowling takes a job as an English teacher in Oporto, Portugal.

1992 Marries Jorge Arantes, a journalism student, on October 16.

1993 Daughter Jessica is born on July 27. Rowling leaves Portugal and moves with her daughter to Edinburgh, Scotland.

1994 Files for divorce from Jorge Arantes.

Begins attending classes at Heriot-Watt University to obtain her teaching certificate. Divorce from Jorge Arantes is finalized on June 26.	**1995**
Christopher Little Literary Agency accepts Rowling as a client.	**1996**
Harry Potter and the Philosopher's Stone is published in England. *Harry Potter and the Philosopher's Stone* wins the Smarties Prize for Children's Literature.	**1997**
Harry Potter and the Chamber of Secrets is published in England. *Harry Potter and the Chamber of Secrets* wins the Smarties Prize for Children's Literature. *Harry Potter and the Sorcerer's Stone* is published in the United States. Warner Brothers Pictures buys the movie rights to *Harry Potter.*	**1998**
Harry Potter and the Chamber of Secrets is published in the United States. *Harry Potter and the Prisoner of Azkaban* is published at the same time in England and in the U.S. *Harry Potter and the Prisoner of Azkaban* wins the Smarties Prize for Children's Literature.	**1999**
Harry Potter and the Goblet of Fire is published.	**2000**
Fantastic Beasts and Where to Find Them and *Quidditch Through the Ages* are published. Movie version of *Harry Potter and the Sorcerer's Stone* is released. Marries Neil Murray on December 26.	**2001**

2002 Movie version of *Harry Potter and the Chamber of Secrets* is released.

2003 Son, David, is born in Edinburgh. *Harry Potter and the Order of the Phoenix* is published.

2004 Movie version of *Harry Potter and the Prisoner of Azkaban* is released.

2005 Daughter Mackenzie is born. *Harry Potter and the Half-Blood Prince* is published. Movie version of *Harry Potter and the Goblet of Fire* is released.

2007 Movie version of *Harry Potter and the Order of the Phoenix* scheduled to premiere.

Chapter Notes

Chapter 1. A Writer's Dream Comes True

1. "Of Magic and Single Motherhood," *Salon*, March 31, 1999 <http://www.salon.com/mwt/feature/1999/03/cov_31featureb. html)> (January 20, 2005).

2. "J.K. Rowling's Diary," *The Sunday Times* (London), July 26, 1998.

3. "Of Magic and Single Motherhood."

4. Lisa DiCarlo, "Harry Potter and the Triumph of Scholastic," *Forbes*, May 9, 2002, <http://www.forbes.com/2002/0509/0509harrypotter.html> (January 20, 2005).

Chapter 2. A House Full of Books

1. Stephen McGinty, "The JK Rowling Story," *The Scotsman*, June 16, 2003 <http://www.news.scotsman.com/archive.cfm?id'662772003> (November 11, 2004).

2. Ibid.

3. Sean Smith, *J.K. Rowling: A Biography* (London: Michael O'Mara Books Limited, 2001) p. 19.

4. J.K. Rowling, "Biography," JK Rowling Official Web site, <http://www. jkrowling.com/textonly/biography.cfm> (February 17, 2005).

5. Danielle Demetriou, "Harry Potter and the Source of Inspiration," *The Daily Telegraph* (London), July 1, 2000.

6. Connie Ann Kirk, *J.K. Rowling: A Biography* (Westport, Conn.: Greenwood Press, 2003), p. 28.

7. Ibid., p. 30.

8. McGinty, "The JK Rowling Story."

9. Linda Richards, "January Profile: J.K. Rowling," <http://www.januarymagazine.com/profiles/jkrowling.html> (November 30, 2005).

10. McGinty, "The JK Rowling Story."

11. "J.K. Rowling: From Single Mom Writer to Global Phenomenon," <http://singleparents.about.com/cs/booksandmovies/1/aajkrowlingbio1.htm> (February 17, 2005).

12. Interview with J.K. Rowling on *CBCNewsWorld: Hot Type*, July 13, 2000, <http://www.cbc.ca/programs/sites/hottype_rowlingcomplete.html> (February 17, 2005).

13. Smith, p. 58.

14. Kirk, p. 39.

15. McGinty, "The JK Rowling Story."

Chapter 3. Becoming a Storyteller

1. J.K. Rowling Official Web site, <http://www.jkrowling.com> (February 18, 2005).

2. Lindsey Fraser, "Harry and Me," *The Scotsman*, November 9, 2002.

3. Sean Smith, *J.K. Rowling: A Biography* (London: Michael O'Mara Books Limited, 2001) p. 84.

4. Stephen McGinty, "The JK Rowling Story," *The Scotsman*, June 16, 2003, <http://news.scotsman.com/print.cfm?id-662772003> (November 11, 2004).

5. Ibid.

6. Fraser, "Harry and Me."

7. Connie Ann Kirk, *J.K. Rowling: A Biography* (Westport, Conn.: Greenwood Press, 2003), pp. 50–51.

8. McGinty, "The JK Rowling Story."

9. J.K. Rowling Official Web site.

10. Fraser, "Harry and Me."

11. Ibid.

12. J.K. Rowling Official Web site.

13. J.K. Rowling, "Multiple Sclerosis Killed My Mother," *Sunday Herald Online* (London), November 16, 2003, <http://www.sundayherald.com/38024> (February 18, 2005).

14. J.K. Rowling Official Web site.

15. Kirk, p. 54.

16. Smith, pp. 101–102.

Chapter 4. Holding Fast to Harry Potter

1. Lindsey Fraser, "Harry and Me," *The Scotsman*, November 9, 2002.

2. J.K. Rowling Official Web site, <http://www.jkrowling.com> (February 18, 2005).

3. Stephen McGinty, "The JK Rowling Story," *The Scotsman*, June 16, 2003, <http://news.scotsman.com/print.cfm?id-662772003> (November 11, 2004).

4. Linda Richards, "January Profile: J.K. Rowling," <http://www.januarymagazine.com/profiles/jkrowling.html> (November 30, 2005).

5. Sean Smith, *J.K. Rowling: A Biography* (London: Michael O'Mara Books Limited, 2001), pp. 115–116.

6. Clare Goldwin, "J.K. Rowling on Her Days of Poverty," *The Daily Mirror* (London), May 20, 2002, <http://www.mirror.co.uk/printable_version.cfm?method'printable_version.html> (February 18, 2005).

7. Rogers, Shelagh. "Interview: J.K. Rowling," Canadian Broadcasting Co., October 23, 2000, <http://www.quick-quote-quill.org/articles/2000/1000-cbc-rogers.htm> (September 15, 2005).

8. J.K. Rowling Official Web site.

9. Jeremy Paxman, Interview with J.K. Rowling, broadcast on BBC Two, June 19, 2003, <http://news.bbc.co.uk/1/hi/entertainment/arts/3004456.stm> (January 19, 2005).

10. McGinty, "The JK Rowling Story."

11. Eddie Gibd, "Tales from a Mother," *Sunday Times* (London), June 29, 1997.

12. Neil Masuda, "Everyone's Just Wild About Harry," *Villarum*, January 2001, p. 13.

13. Alan Cowell, "All Aboard the Potter Express," *New York Times*, July 10, 2000.

14. Smith, pp. 128–129.

15. Roby Macdonald, "Rowling's House of Secrets," *The Scotsman*, March 21, 2004.

16. Ibid.

17. Ibid.

18. Ibid.

Chapter 5. Unexpected Fame

1. Nigel Reynolds, "$100,000 Success Story for Penniless Mother," *The Telegraph* (London), July 7, 1997.

2. J.K. Rowling Official Web site, <http://www.jkrowling.com> (February 18, 2005).

3. Sean Smith, *J.K. Rowling: A Biography* (London: Michael O'Mara Books Limited 2001), p. 134.

4. Anne Johnstone, "Happy Ending, and That's for Beginners," *The Herald* (London), June 24, 1997.

5. Stephen McGinty, "In the Eye of the Storm," *The Scotsman*, June 17, 2003 <http://news.scotsman.com/print.cfm?id-662772003> (November 11, 2004).

6. Shelagh Roger, "Interview: JK Rowling," *Canadian Broadcasting Co.*, October 23, 2000, <http://www.quick-quote-quill.org/articles/2000/1000-cbc-rogers.htm> (September 15, 2005).

7. "J.K. Rowling's Diary," *The Sunday Times* (London), July 26, 1998.

8. "Trivia for Harry Potter and the Sorcerer's Stone," *Internet Movie Database*, 2001, <http://www.imdb.com/title/tt0241527/trivia> (September 16, 2005).

9. Sally Lodge, "Life on the Road," *Publisher's Weekly*, January 14, 1999 <http://www.publishersweekly.com/article/CA166367.html?text'rowling> (January 26, 2005).

Chapter 6. Fame and Fortune

1. Brian Ferguson, "JK Rowling's Fame Spoils Her Café Culture," *The Scotsman*, February 2003.

2. Brian Bethune, "The Rowling Connection: How a Young Toronto Girl's Story Touched an Author's Heart," *Maclean's*, November 6, 2000.

3. Shannon Maughan, "Keeping Up with Harry," *Publisher's Weekly*, November 1, 1999 <http://www.publishersweekly.com/article/ca167516.html?text'rowling> (January 26, 2005).

4. Ibid.

5. Sally Lodge, “On the Road Again,” *Publisher’s Weekly*, December 13, 1999, <http://www.publishersweekly.com/article/CA167693.html?text+rowling> (January 26, 2005).

6. Ibid.

7. Eddie Gibb, “Tales From a Single Mother,” *The Sunday Times* (London), June 29, 1997.

8. Jeremy Paxman, “Newsnight Interview with JK Rowling,” broadcast on BBC Two, June 19, 2003, <http://news.bbc.co.uk/1/hi/entertainment/arts/3004456.stm> (November 10, 2004).

9. Ann Treneman, “Hogwarts and All: The JK Rowling Interview,” *Sunday Herald* (London), June 22, 2003.

10. Nigel Ballard, “JK Rowling Exclusive,” interview broadcast on BBC Bristol, November 12, 2001 <http://www.bbc.co.uk/bristol/content/features/2001/11/12/jk.shtml> (February 15, 2005).

11. “Famous Author Corresponds with Ailing Child,” *Albany Times Union*, December 22, 2002.

12. Fiona Barton and Lesley Yarranton, “Fear Stalks the Hogwarts Express: 24-hour Bodyguards for Harry Potter Author as Obsessive Fan Sends Gifts and Love Notes,” *Mail on Sunday* (London), July 9, 2000.

13. Sally Pook, “JK Rowling Given Honorary Degree at Her Alma Mater,” *The Daily Telegraph* (London), July 15, 2000.

14. J.K. Rowling, “A Kind of Magic,” *The Daily Telegraph* (London), June 9, 2002.

15. “Prince Is Mad About Harry,” *The Times* (London), March 3, 2001.

16. Ibid.

17. "The Queen Meets Two of Britain's Best-Loved Bestsellers," *Daily Telegraph*, March 23, 2001.

18. Rebecca,McQuillan, "Rowling Finds a Meaning in Fame," *Bookshelf*, December 2002.

19. Interview with Richard Curtis on J.K. Rowling's contribution to his Comic Relief Charity, broadcast on Morning Edition (NPR) March 13, 2001.

20. "Harry Gives $1.4 Million," *Toronto Star*, November 25, 2001.

21. Toby MacDonald, "Rowling's House of Secrets," *Scotland on Sunday*, March 21, 2004.

22. Ann Treneman, "Hogwarts and All: The JK Rowling Interview," *Sunday Herald* (London), June 22, 2003.

23. "Press Release: JK Rowling says, 'No Writer's Block,'" *The Scotsman*, October 2001.

Chapter 7. The Work Continues

1. "UK Expels Potter Author 'Stalker,'" CNN.com, <http://archives.cnn.com/2002/SHOWBIZ/books/07/18/rowling.stalker> (February 16, 2005).

2. "Rowling Rows with Neighbours Over Home Security," Thomas Crosby Media, TCM Breaking News, August 30, 2002 <http://archives.tcm.ie/breakingnews/2002/08/30/story66205.asp> (February 16, 2005).

3. "U.S. Pastor Hopes to Snuff Out Harry Potter Influence," *Toronto Star*, December 27, 2001.

4. "Vatican 'No Problems' with Harry Potter," *Catholic News*, February 4, 2003.

5. *Scholastic, Inc., et al.* v. *Stouffer*, 2002 U.S. Dist. LEXIS 17531 (U.S.D.C. SDNY September 17, 2002).

6. "Harry Potter Author Sues Russian Writer for 'Parody,'" *Chicago Tribune*, December 5, 2002.

7. John Pomfret, "It's Harry Potter Versus the Pirates," *International Herald Tribune*, November 2, 2002.

8. Tim Wu, "Harry Potter and the International Order of Copyright: Should Tanya Grotter and the Magic Double Bass Be Banned?" *Slate Magazine*, June 27, 2003 <http:/slate.msn.com/toolbar.aspx?action'print&id-2084960> (February 16, 2005).

9. "US Army in Copyright Investigation Over Harry Potter 'Spoof,'" *Sunday Herald* (London), February 6, 2005.

10. Rebecca McQuillan, "Rowling Finds a Meaning in Fame," *Bookshelf*, December 2002.

11. "Famous Author Corresponds with Ailing Child," *Albany Times Union*, December 22, 2002.

12. Malcolm Jones, "JK Rowling on the New 'Harry Potter,'" *Newsweek*, June 22, 2003.

13. "At the Stroke of Midnight, J.K. Walked In," *The Observer* (London), June 22, 2003.

14. "Villagers Salute JK Rowling's Pounds 200,000 Highland Fling," *The Times* (London), December 1, 2003.

15. Associated Press, "Potter Author Wins Spanish Honor," <http://www.cbsnews.com/stories/2003/09/23/print/main574839.shtml> (February 17, 2005).

16. “Box Office History for Harry Potter Movies,” The Numbers: Box Office Data, <http://www.the-numbers.com/movies/series/HarryPotter.php> (September 16, 2005).

17. “Harry Potter and the Copyright Lawyer,” *Washington Post*, June 18, 2003.

18. Current News, National Council for One Parent Families, <http://www.oneparentfamilies.org.uk> (January 19, 2005).

19. Anita Singh, “Mini Potter Book Nets £11,000 for Charity,” icWales: The National Website of Wales, November 2, 2004, <http://icwales.icnetwork.co.uk?> (January 19, 2005).

20. Jane Bradley, “JK Rowling in £20,000 Donation to Book Centre,” *Edinburgh Evening News*, January 24, 2005.

21. “Harry Potter Launch Magical Night for Wizard’s Army of Fans,” *Edinburgh Evening News*, July 16, 2005.

22. JK Rowling Official Web site <http://www.JKRowling.com> (January 21, 2006).

Chapter 8. When Harry Leaves Hogwarts

1. JK Rowling Official Website <http://www.JKRowling.com> (February 18, 2005).

2. Sean Bullard, Interview with JK Rowling, National Press Club’s author luncheon, October 20, 1999, <http://www.quick-quote-quill.org/articles/1999/1099-presclubtransc.htm> (January 19, 2005).

3. Jeremy Paxman, Interview with JK Rowling, broadcast on BBC Two, June 19, 2003 <http://news.bbc.co.uk/1/hi/entertainment/arts/3004456.stm> (November 11, 2004).

4. Malcolm Jones, “The Return of Harry Potter,” *Newsweek*, July 1, 2000.

5. Jeremy Paxman, Interview with JK Rowling, broadcast on BBC Two, June 19, 2003 <http://news.bbc.co.uk/1/hi/entertainment/arts/3004456.stm> (November 11, 2004).

Further Reading

Beahm, George. *Muggles and Magic: An Unofficial Guide to J. K. Rowling and the Harry Potter Phenomenon.* Charlottesville, Va.: Hampton Roads Publishing Company, 2004.

Chippendale, Lisa A.. *Triumph of the Imagination: The Story of Writer J. K. Rowling.* Philadelphia: Pa., Chelsea House, 2002.

Fraser, Lindsey. *Conversations with J. K. Rowling.* New York: Scholastic, Inc., 2001.

Kirk, Connie Ann. *J. K. Rowling: A Biography.* Westport, Conn.: Greenwood Press, 2003.

Price, Joan. *J. K. Rowling.* Milwaukee, Wisc.: World Almanac Library, 2005.

Sexton, Colleen. *J. K. Rowling.* Minneapolis, Minn.: Lerner Publications, 2005.

Steffens, Bradley. *J. K. Rowling.* San Diego, Calif.: Lucent, 2002.

Internet Addresses

Joanne Rowling's official Web site contains messages from J. K. Rowling, including comments about rumors and scams, and very rare hints about upcoming books.
<http://www.jkrowling.com>

Quick Quotes Quill, an archive of written and audio interviews with J. K. Rowling.
<http://www.quick-quote-quill.org/index2.html>

The Harry Potter Automatic News Aggregator monitors the Internet and collects all news concerning the *Harry Potter* books and movies, including comments, interviews, and graphics of the actors who appear in the movies.
<http://www.hpana.com>

Index

Page numbers for photographs are in **boldface** type.